PRAISE FOR *THE ASHOKAN WAY*

"In this beautiful, elegant, and important book, Gail Straub takes us on a year of walks in the landscape she calls home. But she's really describing a walk we all can take no matter where we live-- the walk that bridges all the landscapes of our being: our connection to place, to each other, to our inner sense of self and outer sense of responsibility to the earth and its peoples. Quoting the ancient I *Ching*, she writes about "coming to rest in motion." She should know: a world traveler and social activist, Gail brings the steady calm she finds in the mountains to her work at peacemaking in a troubled world. "

—ELIZABETH LESSER, NY Times bestselling
author of *Broken Open*

"Walk with Gail Straub in her beloved mountains. Let her take you through the change of seasons, let her show you the altering light and shadow, the dark. You will see all that is visible and all that is not—the mystery that can only be sensed, the kind of beauty that can stun the viewer, or move her to tears. Gail Straub, a part of nature herself, has learned how to lose the static and friction of modern day life, finding a way to live at peace and in balance with nature, accepting the opposites of life and death as part of the Ashokan Way. This is a beautiful and profound book."

—ABIGAIL THOMAS, Bestselling author of *A Three Dog Life*

"What is it to truly come home? Is it not to deeply inhabit the landscapes we are in and to bring all that we are and have been into relationship with them? In *The Ashokan Way* Gail Straub has illuminated this understanding with beauty, respect, and poignancy. She teaches us to look at and inhabit the places we live in, however grand or humble they may be, with total attention and compassion."

—GUNILLA NORRIS, author of *Being Home*

"Nimble and ecumenical in substance, elegant and melodious in style, Straub's prose testifies to how place both elevates and holds our human egos grounded—how listening attentively to its cyclical rhythms keeps our own instruments tuned and humming—ready to serve."

—LISSA KIERNAN, Poet, author of *Glass Needles & Goose Quills*

FOR THE RHYTHM OF COMPASSION

". . . This book is a thorough exploration of the creative and critical tension between action and contemplation. It is a wonderful achievement of the book to disclose so many of the secret bridges between the inner hemisphere of the soul and the outer world of action. Gail's touch is sure as she grounds both worlds critically within the overarching world of narrative. The balance she recommends will be crucial in setting the tonality of our new millennium."

—JOHN O'DONOHUE, author, *Anam-Cara*

"Gail Straub has written a book that addresses with great insight one of the central spiritual questions of our time—how do we care for others while still caring for ourselves? Her book is a must for everyone seeking answers."

—CAROLINE MYSS, author, *Anatomy of the Spirit*

"How many of us have turned away from the ever-present suffering in our troubled world, out of despair and hopelessness about knowing how to help? Gail Straub tackles this issue head-on in this beautiful, wise, and practical book.... Gail speaks with a voice of total authenticity, great compassion, and a seasoned understanding of all the challenges, joys, and dangers that one is likely to encounter along the path of service."

—JOHN WELWOOD, author, *Love and Awakening*

The Ashokan Way

Landscape's Path into Consciousness

The Ashokan Way

Landscape's Path into Consciousness

————————

GAIL STRAUB

Homebound Publications
Ensuring that the mainstream isn't the only stream.

Published in 2018 by Homebound Publications
Front Cover Image and interior images © by Kate McGloughlin
Front Cover Painting is from the collection of Rob and Carla Shultis
Cover and Interior Designed by Leslie M. Browning
ISBN 978-1-947003-69-9
First Edition Trade Paperback

Homebound Publications
Ensuring the mainstream isn't the only stream.

10 9 8 7 6 5 4 3 2 1

Homebound Publications is committed to ecological stewardship. We greatly value the natural environment and invest in environmental conservation. Our books are printed on paper with chain of custody certification from the Forest Stewardship Council, Sustainable Forestry Initiative, and the Program for the Endorsement of Forest Certification.

DEDICATION

*For Joanie, for our early years in the Brandywine River Valley and in Maine.
And for David, for all our years along the Ashokan Way.*

"Although we say that mountains belong to the country,
actually, they belong to those who love them."
—MASTER DŌGEN

"Each form sets a tone, enables a destiny, strikes a note in the universe
unlike any other. How can we ever stop looking?
How can we ever turn away?"
—MARY OLIVER

Table of Contents

FOREWORD

by Stephen Cope

IN THE SPRING OF 1852, a twenty-six-year-old Henry David Thoreau had just finished his two-and-a-half year stint at his cabin on Walden Pond, and was engaged in perhaps the greatest literary challenge of his life. He was revising his greatest work, *Walden: Or, Life in the Woods*, and had come face to face with the central challenge of that book: how to use words to make an energetic connection between the vivid and enchanting world of nature, and the inner world of the human mind and soul.

As we all know, of course, Thoreau succeeded brilliantly, and "nature writing" has never been the same since.

Gail Straub's quiet masterpiece, *The Ashokan Way,* builds on Thoreau's discoveries in every possible way. Her accounts of her daily rambles through her own Catskill Mountain by-ways move effortlessly back and forth between exterior and interior landscapes. We come to know Straub's beautiful inner world as we come to know, too, the very real outer beauties—and occasional terrors—of her mountain home. And, indeed, we come to see how one creates the other.

The Ashokan Way must remind the reader of John Burroughs own extensively chronicled rambles through the self-same Catskill Mountains, or of John Muir's epic relationship with the Sierra Nevada.

But there is something more in Straub's work. It is the factor of time, of movement—of the cycles of the year and their relationship to our inner life. In many ways, Straub does for the

Catskill Mountains what Henry Beston's classic, *The Outermost House* did for the wild beaches at Truro on Cape Cod. It places the human experience in the context of the ebb and flow of the seasons—allowing us to bow for a moment to forces so much more vast than our small selves that we can for a moment feel our right relationship to nature. Just as Thoreau discovered the thrill of "the wild" on Maine's Mount Katadhin, so Straub discovers the thrill of being "right-sized" in the face of awful, wonderful, terrifying, awakening nature.

Toward the end of his life, Thoreau wrote, "I have travelled extensively in Concord." So, too, has Straub travelled extensively on the Ashokan Way. And we are the better for it.

--Stephen Cope
Lenox, Massacusetts

INTRODUCTION

Attention is a form of devotion and a pathway to intimacy. Each day I walk an hour-long loop along the Ashokan Reservoir surrounded by the grandeur of the Catskill Mountain Watershed. Between High Point in the west and Overlook in the east, eighteen peaks encircle the vast reservoir-like ancient bluestone guardians. Bald eagles, red-tailed hawks, great blue herons, leaping trout, and herds of deer are among my regular companions. Occasionally I have human companions too, but the vast majority of my walks are taken alone and used as a time for contemplation and quiet renewal. I've long been enamored that Ashokan translates as the place of many fishes in the Algonkian language, and over the years I have discovered that on every conceivable level this is, indeed, an abundant place. And so I have come to call this daily walk the Ashokan Way, not only because it is a literal walkway, but also because this practice has shaped my way of life.

Though this book tracks one particular year of my rounds, my walkabout has been informed by thirty-six years of strolling through this landscape as well as living in it. For these last decades, I have either been exploring it, observing it from my home, or sleeping and dreaming in a bed that faces directly out onto the Ashokan and her eighteen mountain guardians. I would not be who I am without this body of water and this mountain range. My interior landscape is now so intertwined with this outer landscape that it is impossible to know where one begins and the other ends. Certainly along with my relationships with my husband

David, my family, and my close community of friends, I count my relationship with this place as one of my most cherished. It has shaped me and perhaps, because I have loved it, I have also affected it.

On any given day, walking the Ashokan Way can lead me in any number of directions. Sometimes I am hurled back in time, and the ghosts and voices that haunt this place walk beside me, telling me their stories. Other days the outer landscape takes me deep inside my own territory, trekking the hills and valleys of my aspirations and sorrows, my joys and confusions. On many occasions, this open space offers a profound antidote to my interior terrain that has become overcrowded with distraction and workaholism. And on still other strolls, the land seems to cast me out toward the furthest horizon to a place where I can see through the material into the mystical.

My devotion to the Ashokan Way has opened gateways to mysterious worlds along with portals into self-understanding and restoration. And yet the more intimate I am with these mountains and this water, these forests and creatures, the more I recognize that I will never fully know them. I will never come close to receiving all the benedictions that this landscape has to bestow. Long after I am gone, the Ashokan and the Catskills will still be here. But before my time comes, I want to have written down what they have meant to me. And I hope that in doing this my readers, too, can benefit from the gifts of this place. In giving thanks, I begin and end this tribute on Thanksgiving Day.

WINTER

NOVEMBER

HIGH POINT
MY LIVING MOUNTAIN

Walking on this bright, crisp Thanksgiving Day, I can see High Point's every contour, her gentle hollows and dales along with her stark ridges and plateaus. The soft valleys take my eyes deep into the landscape, while the sharp edges draw my sight back out to the sky. As the clear morning light amplifies the rhythmic inward and outward movement of my gaze, I have the sensation that the entire landmass could be likened to a giant rib cage, with the inner contraction followed by a natural outward expansion. On days when I am very still, I can feel this: the mountain breathing in and breathing out. And with all the leaves gone, the naked outline, the very bone structure of High Point is pronounced. Moving further east, I see the boney formation of the ridges narrowing like a great hand reaching upward toward the summit and once again I have the distinct experience of this mountain as a live being. A dominant influence in my life, this living mountain is my familiar.

Spiritual traditions from all over the world refer to sacred mountains that shape a person's longings and aspirations. Looking back over more than three decades of my life, this is precisely the role that High Point has played. The first time I walked into the small A-frame house that David and I initially rented and eventually owned, I was shocked by the presence of High Point. The mountain loomed so large and so close that I felt like it lived in my tiny kitchen. From that moment of acquaintance in June 1981, the mountain's outline and contours have been omnipresent in my life. And on certain days I still feel like my small

home—perched on a bluestone ridge overlooking the reservoir—
is, in fact, an extension of the mountain itself.

During those first weeks in our house, David and I spent
hours and hours working at our kitchen table. With yellow legal
pads and pens, we alternately planned our wedding and designed
the workshop that would lead to our life's work. Back then we
were still getting used to the fact that every time we looked up
from our work, the imposing presence of a mountain met our
gaze. A few months later on a windy October day, we were mar-
ried in our living room, with High Point as our witness.

Just weeks after we moved to our home, David and I asked
the Woodstock artist Joan Elliot to draw a logo for our new
business. Joan sat on our upper deck and drew a simple sketch
of High Point and the bridge near its base that crosses over the
Ashokan Reservoir. For more than three decades that image has
been the visual symbol for all the work we have done not only in
our small corner of the Hudson Valley, but across North America and in Europe, Asia, Africa, India, and the Middle East. Later,
when we started our small indie press, we called it High Point,
and the impression stamped on all our publications is the unmistakable outline of the mountain that has been such a meaningful
presence in our lives. The iconic image of High Point has come
to represent our marriage and our creative partnership as well as
our individual work and writings. And each and every day the
mountain itself continues to inspire us to give our best to life. It
continues to offer solace and to fortify us in difficult times.

So here I am on this day of giving thanks, walking along the
familiar shores of the Ashokan Reservoir with my mountain
watching me. Today her imposing body stretches out like an im-
moveable mass of ancient rock formation, solid and strong. But
on other days my silent observer becomes a moving river, fluid
and gentle. My eyes trace the familiar outline of this beloved
mountain, aware that both its solidity and fluidity have so much

to teach me, and on this day of thanksgiving, I pause to offer abundant gratitude for its existence in my life.

I used to wonder, as one might with certain close friends, whether I chose High Point as my familiar or if she chose me. Now, after decades of full and fruitful kinship, I feel that we have mutually chosen each other, for at its most essential, friendship is shared presence sustained over time. Surely the potent exchange that creates the lineage of any significant relationship is as mysterious with a mountain as it is with a person. And how blessed is the person who can count among their allies some aspect of the landscape. Let us be grateful then, for that river or tree, that rocky ledge or creature that witnesses our life, offering comfort and joy.

December

MOUNTAIN COMING
TO REST IN MOTION

Just home from a conference and meetings in Washington D.C., I am exhausted, over stimulated, and too full. For me there is only one cure: I need to walk in open space.

Ancient peoples believed that the mountains steadied the earth and held it together. Today as I follow the Ashokan Way, I am certain that the Catskills hold me together. And while the landscape's solidity holds me, the reservoir's waves rock me. My brain feels like an overloaded filing cabinet with the extra files spilling out of my head, tumbling behind me in chaotic heaps. Meanwhile, my footsteps speak: Breathe, empty, space. Breathe, empty, space. Breathe, empty, space.

I listen to my footsteps' counsel and I understand that my challenge is not to eliminate all of the busyness in my life, but rather to empty myself in the midst of the fullness. The *I Ching's* fifty-second hexagram is *Ken*, the mountain majestically moving above and massively still below. The hexagram is described this way: "Ken mountain means coming to rest in motion. When the proper interplay of stillness and action is understood and practiced, the path for progress is bright and glorious." Observing High Point, I see that the peak surrounded by clouds is moving toward heaven while the immense base is the definition of solid motionlessness, earth itself. I long to pull my living mountain inside me so that I might inhabit its balance of action and stillness, heaven and earth.

Ancient wisdom keepers believed that we could better understand the fundamental principles of life when in the presence of a mountain landscape, and this has been true for me. This outer mountain is always ready to help me find my inner mountain. Each day when I leave my office bound up in details and endless lists of things to do, feeling almost buried alive under a torrent of e-mails, I walk into a place that allows me to be empty. For me, this open space is one of the few forces potent enough to overcome the hungry ghosts of modern technological distraction. The landscape returns me to my own inner search engine, reminding me that this interior inquiry is where the roots of my human condition exist. This land reminds me that a computer can never accomplish my internal quest.

Not only does this mountain valley embody the rest in motion that I need, but also it radically alters my sense of time, space, and self. Out here in the open, I feel and sense and think in a different way. Who cares about the minutiae of today's ever-so-important To-do lists when I am surrounded by a landscape formed three hundred million years ago, a place where dinosaurs roamed among primordial plants and massive ice flows carved out mountains as a lasting record of their existence? And here I am, strolling through this valley that silently holds all the memories of past, present, and the eventual future. The long body of this place is humbling, putting all my lists of things to do in their proper perspective. Walking inside this ancient lineage, I will soon find my balance of stillness and action.

The further I go along the Ashokan Way, the more I reside within my inner mountain. All the while, like a giant pitcher of light, this bright day pours its sunshine over the valley's hollows and ridges. It pours and pours its abundant light over me, too. A red-tailed hawk flies just above me, its feathered pattern an intricate mosaic illuminated by the sun. Its strong wings beat away my sense of being overloaded. Higher and higher it soars, way up into all that endless space. My footsteps are nimbler and I feel, for now at least, that I have become the mountain, coming to rest in motion.

Ghosts and Voices
Haunt this Place

After the rain, it's a warm and misty day as shrouds of fog gently settle in the basins of this mountain valley. Like lazy giants, my towering companions are stretched out before me. Mountains from the Burroughs Range—Slide, Cornell, and the Wittenberg—rest next to Lone, Balsam Cap, Rocky, Friday, and Table from the neighboring Bushwack Range. Over the years, David and I have hiked many of these peaks, and they feel like old friends. Along the eagle's peninsula where bald eagles have nested for many years, bare, white birch trees form the boney spine of the forest. Just a few geese still linger on the Ashokan this late in the year before honking off and heading south. On the water the mists are rising up now, following the geese. I am here alone today with all of this silent beauty.

Intoxicated by the untamed loveliness, it's easy to forget that the Ashokan's twelve-mile stretch of open water was artificially created to supply water to one of the world's largest cities. And it's convenient to disregard the thousands of people who had to give up their homes to make way for this reservoir. Most days when I walk here I don't think about these truths, buried in the past as they are. But on some mornings when shrouds of mist mingle with the white bones of trees, the ghosts and voices that haunt this landscape walk right next to me. The people who lived in the towns underneath this place start telling me their stories.

At the turn of the nineteenth century, representatives of the City of New York arrived in the small town of Ashokan to plan for construction of a great dam on the Esopus Creek at Olive

Bridge. Called the last of the handmade dams, the concrete structure was part of the Ashokan Reservoir project, a multimillion-
dollar endeavor that forever changed this valley's way of life as
well as the shape of its land. New York—the fastest growing city
in America at the time—was in what was then called a water fam-
ine, and the city's power brokers were ready to do anything to al-
leviate the dire situation. A private company, the Ramapo Water
Company, was formed by the most influential politicians from
both parties in the state legislature. This coalition eventually se-
cured a power far wider than those of local municipalities, en-
abling it to obtain the water rights throughout the state of New
York. The Ramapo water company acquired the water rights to
build the Ashokan reservoir by simply filing plans with the local
county clerk. The rural people of this valley didn't stand a chance
against the powerful political interests of such an urban force and
soon anger, resentment, and fear thickened the air.

By 1908 the sleepy village of Ashokan had become a modern
town supporting the construction of the dam. More than three
thousand workers lived on the slope of Winchell Hill at Brown's
Station, the encampment built for the laborers.

There were three schools, three churches, numerous brothels, a small hospital, a police station, a firehouse, and a bakery
that produced five thousand loaves of bread a day. Widely diverse
peoples co-existed; Italians, Irish, African-Americans, Russians,
Poles, Swedes, Austrians, and Germans were all part of the mix.
Many of the immigrants didn't speak any English. At night along
with the infamous brawls, cockfights, and mule chariot races, one
smelled cuisine and heard music from multiple corners of the
globe.

But this colorful multinational encampment was not where
the tragedy lived. Ordered by New York City to sell their land,
many of the residents of the Town of Ashokan were given just
ten days notice to pack up and leave their homes forever. Adding

to the shock and horror of dislocation was the fact that they were often paid far less than their land was worth. By 1912 the City of New York had purchased twenty-one thousand acres of land, over fifteen-thousand acres of which were in Ashokan. Nearly two thousand people in Ashokan were forced to leave their homes. Many had farmed their property over multiple generations and so strong was their love of this land that the vast majority resettled within twenty-five miles of the farms they had lost.

And then in 1914 came the blasting and burning away of the towns that would eventually be flooded with the waters of the Ashokan Reservoir: Shokan, West Shokan, Olivebridge, and Olive City among others. Within months the Village of Ashokan, along with its encampment at Brown's Station looked like a ghost town; not even a chimney was left standing. It took nine years to complete the last of the handmade dams, but finally the pure waters of the Catskill Mountains left the giant Ashokan Reservoir and made their way through long aqueducts to New York City. What was a jubilant celebration in the city was an epic loss for the people of this valley.

Close to one-hundred years later, here I am, walking along the shores of lost towns and feeling their echoes and shadows right next to me. Though I can try to ignore the past of this place, the landscape never forgets. The truth is a simple one: the rural communities of the Esopus River Valley were sacrificed for the needs of New York City. The Ashokan Reservoir holds the memory of those lost beneath it, and the mountains surrounding it store the recollections of vanished villages. The old survives alongside the new, a reminder that the inescapable beauty of this place is elegiac.

My Father
White Mountains and Red Blood

It is a heart-stoppingly lovely day. The first heavy snow has fallen and the sky is a piercing cobalt blue. The mountains are wearing white velvet robes as if they are dressed for the finest winter ball, soft clouds settling along their ridges like fur trimming their finery. Snow etches the tree branches as if a paintbrush has outlined each shape with the most delicate of touches. White snow on white birch is silent haiku. As I make my way through the spellbound alabaster landscape, a fierce love for these mountains—for all mountains—rises up in me and I begin to track the long body of my love affair with mountainous terrain all over the world.

My walking pilgrimages have taken me to the Adirondacks, the Alps and the Andes, the High Sierras and the Himalayas, the Rockies and the Red Rock Canyon Lands. My feet have made their paths in the Sahara's Hoggar, the Gennargentu in Sardinia, Gunung Agung in Bali, and Croagh Patrick and Ben Bulben in Ireland. Here at home in the Catskills, what the native Esopus people called the wildcat mountains or the Blue Mountains, my walking has continued to induce that mystical spell that hikers know so well. But the genesis of this lifelong liaison began much earlier in the White Mountains of Maine, where I spent my childhood summers. And the larger truth about my passion for mountainous landscapes is that it's all about my father.

From September through June, my father was a teacher at a private country day school in Wilmington, Delaware. July and August, however, found my Pop—and his family—deep in the

Maine woods, where he helped run a boys summer camp. In the early 1950s, along with some of his Army buddies, my tall, strong father had built the camp's dirt roads and rustic cabins, and in the years following the camp's construction he stayed on as head counselor. Though my sister Joanie and I were girl outliers, my father made sure we learned how to hike alongside to the boys, including our brother Jimmy, and so at an early age Joanie and I knew the strenuous trails of Franconia Ridge, Pinkham Notch, Mount Katahdin, and most demanding of all, Mount Washington. Pop taught us to appreciate the cyclical rhythm of ascent and descent, and how to pace ourselves so that hiking became an extended contemplation. I have long known how fully my father passed on his love of the mountains to me. But it is only now, in my sixth decade, that I have begun to understand the fuller connection between my father and mountains.

Many evenings during those Maine summers, I would sit silently next to my Pop as we looked out over Kimball Pond and the White Mountains. Sunset colors would mix with the comforting smell of the pipe that he smoked in relaxed moments like this. Our silence was intimate, and even as a girl I knew the mountains were my father's church. Though my mother dragged him to Catholic Mass every Sunday, I fully understood what was sacred to my father. I understand now that as we sat quietly in the company of the pond and the mountains we were praying. And I see why this was the only place that my father could pray. As a twelve-year-old boy, after watching his own father take a gun to his head during the Great Depression, what other God could my Pop ever trust but a steady, unshakable mountain range? My Pop spoke of father's death only a single time during his lifetime, words spoken aloud just once, but unspoken each and every day. My father's abiding strength of character was forged in the fires of suffering.

I never got to ask my Pop all the questions that still haunt me twenty-five years after his death. Did your father's blood spill all over you? Did your mother comfort you, or did you hold her? Who cleaned up the unthinkable mess and how did you ever go on? Was it the constant presence of this trauma that made you determined to shape such a meaningful life for our family?

As a boy, my Pop had already lost his sister to tuberculosis by the time his father killed himself. And then when he was sixty-five, he lost his wife—my mother—the love of his life. Just when all his children were out of the nest and they could have enjoyed their later years together, she was taken from him and he was alone. The Sanskrit word for mountain is a-ga, meaning "that which does not go." The White Mountains were a-ga for my father. And until he died at eighty-one years, my father was a-ga for me with his solid and constant presence. Now this mountain valley is a-ga for me. And each day, this place where I pray connects me to my father.

Now my tears mix with my father's tears, and the solace so freely given by the White Mountains merges with that given by the Catskills here along the Ashokan Way. Is it always that the deepest sadness is most bearable in the company of the greatest beauty? These white, snow-covered mountains have allowed me to honor my grandfather's spilled red blood and the strength of my father that was forged in that blood. And my love of these peaks is forever linked with my love for my Pop.

January

EXACTLY WHO IS WITNESSING
ALL THIS BEAUTY?

I am here alone with a day so mild that dense mists pour off the snow banks. Following the rising vapors for almost a mile, I feel as if I am riding a great rolling wave. Soon cloaked in the white mists myself, I become part of this moving current. The mountains are rendered utterly invisible by this thick fog, but when the wind blows, it opens small portals of visibility into the valley, like a window being cleared of condensation. As the wind picks up, it opens and closes more portals, as if shutters were being rapidly flung open and then shut along the mountain range. The wind has become a deft magician, performing sleight of hand with the visible and invisible. Are the mountains really there or am I just imagining them? And then a question fills my mind, one that I have often pondered when I am out in the landscape: Exactly who is witnessing all this beauty?

As I walk further into the fluctuating terrain, the sun breaks through as bright patches of blue dot the sky. I can feel the sunshine melting my misty cloak as it spreads its warmth over the landscape. Gradually, in slow motion, the entire heavy blanket of fog rises off this bluestone range almost as if a painter was lifting a veil to reveal a masterpiece. Up, up, the mists lift higher and higher revealing the bases of the massive mountains surrounding me. And then slowly, inexorably, all eighteen peaks appear before my eyes, like giant newborns. I stand transfixed, as if I am seeing this mountain valley for the first time. And some veil is also lifted off me too, because witnessing such unexpected splendor alters a person forever.

Is such revelation accidental? There is not another person in sight and I can't help but wonder whether this entire spectacle was a private showing just for me. It's highly unlikely that I will see this precise combination of elemental magic again in my lifetime. These mists that I have ridden like a great wave, this wind that is a deft magician, this sunlight that transformed the valley into a newborn baby—what are they telling me? Landscape illusionists, they remind me that though there is a worthy place for will and reason in this life, there is an equally important role for the inexplicable and the miraculous. Remembering that there are ways of seeing and knowing that cannot be summoned by my will or understood by my mind is a great gift, perhaps even a salvation. I want to bow down to the mist, the wind, and the light. I want to tell them how grateful I am for this benediction that has left me rearranged.

Recalling Rilke's line "There is no place at all that is not looking at you," I wonder if the three elemental tricksters have been watching me as carefully as I have been watching them. Rilke joins a long line of poets, mystics, and shamans who believe in this mutual exchange between humans and the landscape. Is it possible then, that my genuine awe and gratitude for the beauty that the elements conjured today has offered them an unexpected revelation? There is no way to know this for sure. But in my heart I feel that my walk this morning was a miracle witnessed by both myself and by the landscape. And that such unheralded moments of marvel are not just for humans alone.

Praying in the Cathedral
of the Ashokan

My Mother and Faith

O n this cold January day the mountains stride boldly across
the blue sky wearing their winter whites. Outlined by fresh
snow, the trees are backlit by brilliant sunshine. Upon this luminous, pearly backdrop, a flock of hundreds of tiny dark-eyed
juncos appear as a delicate black-lace pattern in flight. Here I am
on my birthday, walking through the mountain cathedral I have
been attending for thirty-six of my sixty-eight years. Here I am
in this sacred landscape where I have released my exhaustion and
overload, found solace and renewed perspective, remembered
who I am, and birthed most of my good ideas. This is my church
and there is no place I love more. Walking here on this day of
my birth, I find myself thinking about my faith and about my
mother.

A fervent Irish Catholic, Mom made sure our family went to
Mass at St. Joseph's Church every Sunday of my childhood without fail. Indeed, after receiving the sacraments of Holy Communion and Confirmation, I diligently attended both confession
and Mass every week for years—until, that is, at age eighteen,
I went off to college where I studied Marxism and later wor-
shipped in the church of sex, drugs, and rock and roll.

At the time what I liked most about those Sundays at St.
Joseph's was the quiet time for praying, the consistency of the
weekly ritual, and the intimacy of my mother sitting close to me,

always elegant in her Sunday best, her Dior perfume mixing with the pungent church incense. But the full impact of those years of weekly mass is the lasting imprint of my mother's faith on me. It was such an intrinsic part of who she was that it eventually became an intrinsic part of who I am, albeit in a slightly different form. Her mystical bent grounded in a devout prayer life; her heightened appreciation for beauty, which she considered a form of prayer; her capacity to sustain her conviction in the face of great challenges, most especially her fragile health; her courage to carry the presence of death on her shoulder; and last but not at all least, her enormous confidence that I could do anything and be anyone—all these things were facets of her deep and abiding faith, and to say that I would be nothing without them only hints at their significance.

My mother died when she was fifty-five, so at sixty-eight, I have now enjoyed thirteen more years of life than my mother was given. I used to fear how deeply disappointed she would be at my failure to be a good Catholic. But now I believe that Mom would understand that my church is this place in the mountains, where daily I say the rosary, praying for those I love along with those who need support. I feel confident that what I experience here in the Ashokan Cathedral is not so different from what she experienced sitting in the pews at St. Joseph's Church: solace in difficult times, an abiding conviction in something inexplicable but good, encouragement to live a kind and full life, and the belief that death is a friend. I finally see that we can never know exactly what form the early kernels of faith will blossom into. But more essential than the form itself, the original spiritual seeds that my mother so carefully planted have borne fruit in me, evidenced in my capacity to deepen and sustain my faith over the course of my lifetime.

So today, walking along the reservoir, on the anniversary of the morning sixty-eight years ago when she gave birth to me, I am moved to proclaim right out loud, "I am my mother's daughter!" On this cold January day of my birth, I feel warm and filled with grace. Suddenly I know that the flock of dark- eyed juncos I saw earlier was a birthday blessing from Mom. And that my memory of her is like those birds, a luminous lace pattern in flight held high aloft by the wind.

A Walk with John Burroughs
Appreciating Winter's Gifts

The molten sky with its subtle shades of gray is just waiting for the snow to arrive. Soon the quiet space opens my seeing and I recognize the red-tailed hawk sitting motionless high up in the leafless trees. Her feathered camouflage so precisely matches the hardwood forest that I only find her when I am still inside. From her lofty perch she surveys the wide sweep of the valley's mountains, water, and sky.

The snow begins, amplifying my wordless communion with the hawk. Within our quietude I feel I can almost hear the fluffy white flakes falling, coating me with their benediction. My love for winter comes over me with such an unexpected force that tears spring from my eyes. How fond I am of the alabaster landscape, the stark naked shapes of the trees, the way the cold clears my head, the incomparable silence after a snowstorm. How I love the fact that everything seems so much simpler in this season. Winter demands more of us, but in return for our appreciation, it has so much to offer. I start to walk again, putting down tracks, getting snow drunk.

Of all the writings of the Hudson Valley nature mystic John Burroughs, it is his descriptions of winter that speak to me most deeply, including this passage from *In the Catskills*.

"The simplicity of winter has a deep moral," he writes, "The return of nature, after such a career of splendor and prodigality, to habits so simple and austere, is not lost either upon the head or the heart. It is the philosopher coming back from the banquet and the wine to a cup of water and a crust of bread."

"Yes," I think. "That is just how I feel." After the abundant sensual feast of the fall, the zen simplicity of winter is a great relief. Its emptiness offers the natural counterpart to such fullness. This cycle's soft shades of grey calm me. With the bare bones of the landscape now accentuated, I, too, am invited to get down to the bones of things. My mind has more space and my thoughts can spread out. As my entire psyche turns inward, my interior life begins its richest season. Like a stew simmering on the woodstove, my creative projects cook during these months. The longer periods to think, read, and write leave my mind disciplined and sharp, my body resolved to act when the warmer days arrive. After an arduous period of mental concentration, it's pure joy to go outside into the cold air and empty the mind once again. And for me there is no greater winter pleasure than to walk out into the snow.

And now it's snowing hard and I have a paradoxical sensation that the cold snow forms a warm blanket for this mountain valley. Utterly democratic, the whirling flakes transform every inch of the landscape. The snow owns this entire place, like a benevolent ruler who just suddenly showed up. Sounds are magnified in the luminous quiet: the crunching of my footsteps, the clumps of snow falling from the tree branches, and the wind rustling through the forest like woodland chimes. I can imagine John Burroughs walking next to me exclaiming how "the world lies about in a trance of snow!" Or the old white-bearded mystic might be pointing out the tracks of deer or hawks, calling them "the snow walkers." And I am a snow walker too, transported by the marvel of falling flakes. Now fully garbed in immaculate white, I open my arms grateful to receive the gifts of winter: a season to simplify and return to the bones of my life; a period to enrich my interior life through reflection, reading, and writing; and a time to create new ideas with a quiet clear mind.

FEBRUARY

SHAPE SHIFTING,
SNOW DESERT TO THE SAHARA

For over a week the weather has been frigid and now large stretches of the reservoir are frozen solid. The fierce wind blowing off the ice almost convinces me to turn around and head for home. But I know that with the current at my back the going will be easier on my return, so I forge ahead hunched against the cold. The wind above is making high-pitched tones like a soprano's voice, and the groaning ice below sounds like a bass. The stronger the wind is, the louder the moaning beneath the frozen landscape. Soon the unearthly duet sounds to me like the howling of ghosts, and I sense these haunted voices can only be the souls underneath the ice who lost their homes when the Ashokan was constructed. Their piercing cries are colder than the cold itself.

When I finally turn around to head home, my walk is utterly transformed. With the wind to my advantage, I can be present to the valley's beauty. This morning's freshly fallen powder has rendered vast stretches of the reservoir into a dazzling snowy desert, and strong gusts blow the snow into dense whiteouts, the frozen analog of a giant sandstorm. Caught inside the swirling white, I am catapulted by this frigid tundra landscape into its most extreme contrast.

Sometimes sense memories of a landscape visited long ago remain in your psyche, appearing in your dreams, intent on teaching you something that you have not yet grasped. Four decades ago at the end of my Peace Corps service in West Africa, I crossed the Sahara Desert with Tuareg nomads on their camel caravan. A young woman of twenty-three, I was the only foreigner, and all these years later, the images of the Tuareg along with their desert culture can come upon me without warning as if I were still there. What, exactly, is the Sahara trying to teach me?

Before embarking on the month-long journey north across Niger into the Hoggar Mountain Range leading to Northern Algeria, I made my preparations in Agadez, at the southwestern corner of Niger. A small paradise of artistry, the Agadez market was vibrant with Tuareg women weaving intricate straw mats, decorating pottery vessels, and designing brightly-colored leather-camel saddles. And camels were absolutely everywhere! I was given my desert clothes—an airy, floor-length black robe embroidered with complex white symbols, and a high black turban that covered my face and head against the relentless Sahara sun. When dressed, I felt both light and closed in; only my eyes peeked out from a tiny slit in my turban. Later, I experienced the legendary Bedouin generosity when an elderly Tuareg woman offered me a beautiful, old, silver-Tuareg cross as protection in the desert.

Soon there were fourteen of us lined up in our caravan with goatskins full of water slung by our sides. With each passing day, our camels carried us farther into the Sahara, and I fell more deeply under the spell of the Tuareg women who protected me and taught me about their culture. Regal beyond description, these nomads stood more than six feet tall and had intricate henna patterns full of spiritual symbolism covering much of their bodies. I quickly learned that the women controlled all mediums of magic and medicine, using intricate herbal formulas for birth control. And it was the Bedouin women who were the masters of poetry, music, and the trance dances used to ward off evil spirits. Gliding across the desert with their long robes of flowing folds, great turbans of white, black, and indigo, the Tuareg women seemed to float just above the sand as if they were mirages. It is especially these women who still inhabit my dreamscape.

Like most indigenous peoples, the Tuaregs were intimately

connected with the natural world's mysterious forces. The nomads could sense a sandstorm coming days before it arrived, re-
lied solely on the stars to navigate the endless Sahara, and were
so familiar with each of their camels that they could recognize
illness by simply touching the creature.

Traversing countless miles of sand, our camels took us into
the towering mountains of the Mouydir. The dark peaks seemed
to spring out of nowhere, jagged with sliced- off tops, unearthly
as if we had landed on the moon. Penetrating black presences
against the vast stretches of white, they beckoned in an irrefut-
able way. There was no green anywhere except when we came
upon an oasis, each one a surreal little pocket in the middle of
the stark terrain. Stunning in the contrast they provided, the lush
oases were replete with waterfalls, and date, fig, orange, and lem-
on trees. Mint grew in fragrant profusion, and magenta orchids
flooded the sides of the streams, giving the illusion that the water
was on fire.

In the evenings we drank strong smoky tea as we all lay cradled
in the sand under avalanches of stars so close that they seemed to
pour over us. Long into the night, the Tuareg recited songs, stories, and poetry in their complex language, creations filled with
images of camel caravans, desert plants, sandstorms, and lovers
embracing. The high shrill tone of the women's voices pierced
the stillness. The sound of the calabash, a large gourd filled with
water and played like a string instrument, was as glorious as any
Bach cello suite. The sheer force of the nomads' music bursting
out into the immensity of the Sahara sometimes caused me to
weep. Time as I knew it had utterly disappeared into this vast
space.

And now this memory of the Tuareg voices and the strings
of the calabash opens a portal inside me. At the time I crossed
the desert it had been barely six months since my mother's death.
Though unexpressed, my grief was at the very forefront of my

heart and everything about the Bedouin women connected me
to my mother's essence: their artistry and refined sense of beauty,
their mysticism and maternal protection, their strength balanced
with tenderness. I feel certain now that the recurring images of
the Sahara and the Tuareg women are messages from my mother.
"Remember these characteristics are both my essence and yours.
Remember that a life without these qualities is not worth living,"
she is saying to me. Like my time in the Sahara, my time with
my mother was too short, but like my memory of the desert, her
memory is ever present for me.

Now the frigid wind and the howling ghosts beneath the frozen Ashokan bring me back to this day and this place. I have the
distinct sensation of reappearing after having disappeared inside
the snowy whiteout. Once again the landscape has radically al-
tered my sense of time and dimension, rendering me uncertain
which is more real—the sandstorm in the Sahara, or the snowstorm here on the Ashokan? But today both have led me back
to my mother. And perhaps, unintentionally, I have done what
the desert mystic Hafez once suggested: "Follow the tracks in the
sand that lead beyond thought and space."

THAT WHICH IS EVIDENT
IS ALSO MYSTERIOUS

Snow squalls gust across the valley as the entire landmass is swallowed by white. The light has vanished and the mountains have totally disappeared. When the snow stops, the sky bursts through like bright blue patchwork and the peaks reappear like satisfied tricksters. After ten minutes, this cycle repeats itself. At one moment a squall renders the landscape utterly invisible and I can hardly see, and in the next, the mountain range is fully visible, concrete, and bathed in light. Moved by this interplay between light and then dark, visible and then invisible, I wonder how this exchange occurs inside me, too.

Yugen, the Chinese character for mystery, is also the sign for mountain. Yugen is inscribed like an inverted T with the straight vertical line representing the mountain, that which is evident and constant. The horizontal lines on each side signify the snow or mist in the valley, that which is hidden and mysterious. In true Taoist fashion, the evident is always accompanied by the mysterious.

Just as I am contemplating the paradox of yugen, a much stronger squall stampedes across the land, filling the basin. Once again I am engulfed in a vortex of giant snowflakes and fierce wind gusts. Once again the mountains, sky, forests, and reservoir cease to exist. I tumble within this wild tempest. Absorbed by the squall, I have also disappeared, invisible to the world. I stop moving on my own accord, allowing the wind to take me. The lack of visibility leaves me feeling disoriented but also profoundly energized. Inside the swirling white vortex I lose all sense of time and space. And then just as abruptly as it arrived, the squall departs.

Once again the familiar terrain takes shape and I reappear in human form. During the course of my walk this metaphysical drama
repeats itself two more times; I become invisible, swallowed up
by snow and wind, and then returned to form, engulfed in warm
sun and on familiar ground.

Moving between the elements' vital contrasts has rendered
me radically awake and realizing how much teaching is embedded in the vast changes I have just passed through. The landscape demonstrated clearly and precisely how to surrender to the
unknown, trusting that familiar ground will eventually return.
And I experienced how much vitality is available when I can shift
back and forth between light and dark, visible and invisible, concrete and transparent. After spinning around inside the *yugen* of
this particular mountain valley, I have a visceral understanding
of how everything that is evident to me is also mysterious. My
cherished husband David, my dearest friends, my remarkable
colleagues in distant corners of the globe, all of them are familiar
to me, but also they frequently surprise me. I want to be equally
hospitable to both their visible and invisible aspects. Even to myself, I am both evident and mysterious, possessing my own *yugen*;
I contain both the vertical constancy of my inner mountain along
with misty hidden valleys. Sometimes my unexpected responses
or actions, either positive or negative, can leave me wondering
just who I am. Indeed, I sometimes disappear inside an untamed
squall that blows across the familiar landscape of my own being.
The Ashokan Way is guiding me to welcome those unexpected
moments as vital and revelatory.

Meanwhile, the shape-shifting squalls have lifted and a cobalt
sky frames a mountain range that is as familiar to me as the sil-
houette of my own face.

LOON CALL

This week's warm weather has broken up much of the Ashokan's frozen tundra. An azure sky and puffy clouds are precisely reflected in a giant opening in the reservoir, giving the impression that the blue earth is being held by an immense mosaic of cracked ice. As the day turns even milder, delicate mists begin to puff off the snow banks. I want to inhale these vapors, sensing that they offer some sort of ephemeral elixir. Suddenly, I hear the call of loons, and I see a pair of them floating on the reservoir in the enormous hole in the ice. Their song is singular, both otherworldly and profoundly inviting.

Loons awakened me many summer mornings of my childhood. Across Kimball Pond their inimitable calls came wafting, perfectly bridging the realm of sleeping and the world of waking. Some mornings, when there was a thick fog on the pond, their song seemed to arise from haunted phantoms living deep beneath the water's surface. But when the day dawned bright and clear, their voices were among the most welcoming sounds I had ever heard. Lying in my bed in our cabin in the Maine woods, I could listen to the loon chant for a long, long time, echoing back and forth as it did like choral call and response. I loved the loons' refrain beyond any understanding that my rational brain could clarify, but even as a young girl I sensed their birdsong was a gateway into something essential, something that would shape the rest of my life. Even then I intuited that encoded in the loon's call was the message that contact with the wild could set me free.

Now in my late-sixties, I have more words for what I instinctively knew as a girl. I understand how the landscape allows me to feel part of an intricate evolutionary design, both enlarging me while simultaneously rendering me insignificant. Living within the tension of these opposites helps free me as a human creature. Nature constantly demonstrates that this path to freedom is a vital and demanding spiritual journey. Patient and ever present, the natural world is always available to help me with this journey. Thus my daily walks along the Ashokan Way reflect the phases of spiritual practice that can lead to liberation: exile, return, and belong.

As I begin my daily walking meditations, all too often I am exiled from my natural state. Stressed, self-absorbed, and separate, I find myself imprisoned by the small bounded world of my ego. But entering the landscape, I am soon returned to consciousness, awake to the larger web of life of which I am a part. An awareness of the mountains, water, forests, or the call of loons—any of these can bring me back to mindfulness, and a sense of myself as part of a much larger whole. My focused attention to some specific aspect of nature quiets the chatter in my mind and I feel less isolated and more connected. By the end of the hour-long walk my equilibrium and sense of self have been restored. My mind has emptied, my life is clearer, and I am no longer separate from myself nor from the greater cosmos. I am both smaller and larger. Nature has returned me to my natural state of belonging, the place where my deepest liberation resides.

Now as I end my walk on this bright February day, the loon chant traveling across the Ashokan Reservoir reminds me that I am always welcome to move through exile, to return to myself, and to belong to something larger. And the loons' echoing call says the same thing to me today as it did more than fifty years ago when I was a young girl in the Maine woods: *I am natural, I am wild, and I am free. I am natural, I am wild, and I am free.*

SPRING

MARCH

QUEEN EAGLE AND WOMEN OF THE GLOBE
FOR WHAT HAVE WE BEEN PUT ON THIS EARTH?

It's that moment in time when we are suspended between winter's end and spring's beginning. The high peaks are covered
in fresh snow while the valley below is brown and the birds are
beginning to sing. Even the Ashokan's melting ice floes appear
like giant petals waiting to open. And, something that thrills me
when I see and hear it: the pair of bald eagles that have made this
spot on the reservoir their home are shoring up their nest.

Today I watch as the male flies overhead, his massive talons
trailing long tufts of dried-brown grass. Further on I hear the
unmistakable high-pitched squeals echoing back and forth that
tell me the eagles are mating. Listening to their romantic duet,
I reflect on how blessed this valley is to have them as an integral
part of the community. And I am glad that this spot along the
Ashokan Way has been deemed an official site for their protection. For fifteen years now, they've nested high up in the massive
evergreens on the far end of a particularly beautiful birch-filled
peninsula. Once the eggs are laid, the female eagle sits on the nest
for thirty-five days while the male brings her ample fresh fish and
other food fit for a queen. During this time, a kind of reverence
falls over the Ashokan Way, as those of us doing our daily walks
here await the birth of the baby eagle or eagles. For many of us, it's
a highly-anticipated event.

It is no surprise that my psyche is replete with images of the
queen eagle on her nest, her eggs are harbingers of birth, because
today is International Women's Day and I have spent the last

few days in New York at the United Nations Commission on the Status of Women. Thousands of women from all over the globe convened to discuss a dizzying array of topics, including the major impact of gender equality on global economic stability, environmental sustainability, national security, terrorism prevention, population control, and ending violence against women. As I walk today, the faces of my sisters—friends and colleagues from India, Africa, and the Middle East, as well as women I have just met—fill my consciousness. Each day they face the harshest challenges: limited resources, lack of stable infrastructure, lives spent in war zones, ostracism from society, and for some, death threats because of the work they are doing to empower women. And yet there they are, every day all over the globe, out in the chaotic urban streets or the dusty rural villages, heads held high wearing their bright headscarves, turbans, and saris. There they are in the sprawling city slums, in the dark trenches of the brothels, or in the safe houses they run. Their courage and passion give me a strength that I never knew I had. As much as anything in my life these women have changed me for the better, pushing me out of my comfort zone and demanding that I reflect on what really matters. Often we think it's the affluent Global North giving to the underdeveloped Global South, but the truth is that it's a dynamic mutual exchange.

Turning to face Indian Head and Overlook, I fling open the gates of my imagination to find a magnificent archetypal woman formed by the elements. The snowy mountain peaks create her towering white turban, a round ice-covered cove is her head, the cracked ice mosaic at the cove's end is her shimmering necklace, and the open waters of the Ashokan become her flowing regal robe. Her strong feet are formed from the rocky shore. The wind is robust now, and the reservoir's waves create the impression of a blue batik pattern in her swirling robe. There she stands tall before me, this giant of a woman made from mountains, ice, water, wind, and, rock.

Here in the presence of this elemental goddess, I am thinking of my Afghan colleague, whom I will call Soraya, who spoke yesterday at the United Nations. Like this landscape woman, Soraya stands tall, though her days are difficult. She faces repeated trials that are clearly designed to cut her down to a smaller size—the size of a woman without the vision and determination to make life better for the people of Afghanistan. She runs innovative safe houses for women in chaotic cities and remote villages who have experienced an unspeakable array of acts, and for Afghan men too, because she understands that the entire family needs to be healed if her country is going to move forward. Numerous death threats have been made on her life, and sometimes the threats are followed by action. A car bomb once left her unharmed, but totally destroyed her vehicle leaving body parts from the car in front of her splattered all over her windshield. Now Soraya has bodyguards and, on a happier note, a loving and supportive husband and several rambunctious children. When I asked Soraya how she kept going and if she ever wanted an easier life, she said, "Those aren't really the right questions to ask me. Ask me why I do this and then I can tell you that this work is what I am made for, this is what I have been put on this earth for. If I lived an easier life where I wasn't doing this work, I would just be a shadow of myself. I would prefer to lose my life having lived as a full person rather than having lived safely as a ghost of myself."

Now, looking out at the mighty woman made from mountains, ice, water, wind, and rock, I pray that I am living as a full person. And I invite these primal elements to offer their benedictions to Soraya and all the bold women in their colorful headscarves, turbans, and saris whose company I have just shared. May these mountains and rocks bestow upon my courageous sisters' physical fortitude. May these waters grant them emotional stamina. And may the wind confer upon them a resilient spirit. When once again I hear the Queen Eagle's high-pitched sounds way out on the birch-filled peninsula, I ask that her birdsong impart a final blessing. May we all live the lives for which we have been put on this earth.

THE SPRING EQUINOX
ON LANDSCAPE AND FAITH

Here on the Ashokan Way, spring equinox is heralded by six inches of fresh snow with almost a foot of powder up in the higher elevations: the mountains have donned their white velvet robes yet again, perhaps headed to the final winter ball of the season. But nestled on her eggs, mother eagle reminds us that though this valley is still dressed in winter's finest garb, spring is, in fact, around the corner. Squinting, I can imagine the haze of red buds that will soon transform this land in the most dramatic fashion. All through the cold months this white tundra has been pregnant with these red buds. On this windy, snowy equinox I know that this stark landscape will soon give birth to what is now utterly invisible: a multitude of sprouted seeds and exploding chartreuse blossoms, chirping baby birds and fragile newborn fawns, flowers in yellows, purples, and magentas so vivid that they leave me forgetting what snow feels like.

Why is my faith in nature's inexorable progression so strong, while my trust in the commensurate metaphysical process in my own life so weak? While I have complete confidence that the landscape's invisible seeds will inevitably bloom, I struggle mightily to believe that the unseen kernels of my own visions will manifest. The law of future creation, as understood in metaphysics, states that with fervent and abiding intention, with careful weeding and watering, what is now invisible will become visible. But alas, in my daily life I find it difficult to trust the dictum "As above, so below."

In my daily work, I sow the kernels of social change through women's empowerment initiatives in Africa, India, and the Middle East. I want to believe that once I have carefully planted these seeds, continuing to tend them like a good gardener, then I can trust that these endeavors will come to fruition. But I worry far too much, and I demand that my efforts manifest quickly. Hounded by impatience, I try to control the timing and the way in which my intentions unfold. And underneath my worry and desire for control, lie my deepest fears: that I can never do enough, and that whatever I accomplish, it might already be too late to effect change. My ego battles against these fears, begging for assurance that my actions will turn out the way I think they should. But my ego's constant effort and strain is grinding me down. And as I grow older I have come to see that this self-important willfulness serves neither me, nor my endeavors. How on earth though, do I put this knowledge into practice?

Out here in the open space of sky, water, mountains, and forest, I am held by an ancient visceral rhythm. Nature offers me its steady presence, its ongoing surrender to the unknown; it also extends its hospitality equally toward life and death. Throughout their cycles, the seasons demonstrate a unified affinity between what is known and visible and what is unknown and invisible. And the graceful seasonal tempo between living and dying is natural and comforting. Each year I witness winter's pregnant emptiness followed by the bursting forth of spring's young fullness, which in turn gives way to summer's mature presence. Finally, autumn announces the beginning of emptiness and the natural movement toward death. In this moment I am once again struck by how true to itself the natural world is.

Today I understand that truthfulness, or being true to oneself, is intrinsic to faith, and it can help me let go of my need to tightly control outcomes. If I am true to myself, giving my gifts to the world as best I can, my ego softens and faith replaces worry.

In this softer, truer place, I accept that the work of social change will never be finished. The inexorable seasons of changing the world will continue to unfold. Long after I am gone people will take up where I have left off, and true to themselves, they will plant their own seeds and garden as skillfully as they can. Their fullness will replace my emptiness. It is this understanding that I want to pass on to those who will continue the work that I have started. I want them to know that by being true to themselves, they will also find an abiding faith in the unfolding of life.

Just a few miles from where I stand, Abbot John Daido Loori wrote about this at the Mount Tremper Zen Monastery.

The great earth innocently
nurtures the flowers of spring.
Birds trust freely
the strength of the wind.
All this derives from the power of giving,
as does our self, coming into being.

Just like today's spring equinox, this time when light and dark are in balance, I want my faith to abide in the fertile territory between the stark-white winter tundra of right now, and the imminent arrival of spring's blaze of red buds. I want my faith to rejoice in this potent tension between what I know to be real and visible right now, and the invisible possibility that is the future. And I want my faith to welcome the natural unfurling of my life's seasons as they move from fullness to emptiness.

Easter Sunday
The Sanctuary of Landscape and Community

On this clear and cold Easter morning, I am greeted by a gregarious gathering of the winged community. Some of the woodpeckers, phoebes, robins, crows, and dark-eyed juncos flying overhead sing loudly; others grasp small twigs and tufts of dead grass with which to build their nests. The geese have also come honking back, getting ready to nestle down. And from the fresh Ashokan waters, papa eagle catches shimmering silver fish with which to nourish expectant mama, who has just a few more weeks before her eggs will hatch. The trees, too, are expecting, with their haze of pink buds before the bursting of greenery. Each year I eagerly anticipate the mist of tiny red blossoms that spreads across the lower mountain valley like a rosy watercolor released into the landscape. In the company of this water and sky, these mountains, forests, and creatures, I feel a profound sense of sanctuary.

As I walk this morning, I find myself reflecting on the close relationship between landscape as sanctuary and community as sanctuary. What quality is it that allows both of these to become a refuge, and why is this so important? In a few hours David and I will host twelve dear friends for our Sacred Circle gathering. For over two decades this group has been meeting four times a year to bear witness to each other's lives. Through the most joyful and the most difficult times—marriage and divorce; birth and death; cancer and Parkinson's; the release of books, CDs, art, and films into the world—we have created the refuge of community for one another. Each time we meet, we create a beautiful hand-made program that lays out a simple but intentional rhythm. An

inspirational opening passage is read aloud followed by music
that takes us into a forty-five minute silent meditation. Another
piece of music brings us out of meditation and into Quaker style
sharing. After being taken deep inside by the meditation, we are
able to speak from our hearts without interruption or cross conversation. Across these many years of sharing, our dreams and
disappointments have unfurled like flocks of birds, coming and
going in the open sky. Like the open sky, the community witnesses the passages of our lives with gentle constancy. We close
with a prayer or poem followed by a potluck feast, where the rich
food and conversation often lasts for hours.

On this Easter Sunday, I begin with the first paragraph of
Khalil Gibran 's passage on friendship from his classic work *The
Prophet.*

> *Your friend is your needs answered.*
> *He is your field which you sow with love*
> *and reap with thanksgiving.*
> *And he is your board and your fireside.*
> *For you come to him with your hunger,*
> *and you seek him for peace.*

The Catskill Mountain Air for High Point opens our meditation and Jay Unger and Molly Mason's beloved Ashokan Farewell brings us out of the silence. After our sharing, we end our
gathering with a reading of a poem entitled *Remember This* by my
sister Joanie McLean—Joanie, a poet and wetlands farmer, and
my constant childhood companion in exploring the land and listening to loons.

Remember this:
that you walked toward the waxing moon's
neap tide as it laughed and roared
up from the ocean floor

that the green—no, the blue—no, brown...
leapt and tore at the beach
as you came

that it was October—the month that throws you
down, prostrates you before its galloping bent towards
rot and darkness

that an osprey beat and pined against the wind,
tilted and tilted, showed you her white throat
then was driven down so close you caught her gaze.

Remember that you had been old until then—
held, until then, to your words
and your bones.

And remember that while you stood at the top of the dune
the tide turned and each wave
held the light a little longer

and no one's words mattered any more.
They'd all been said and none of them
was the tide or the light or the osprey's flight.

Surrounded by my community of beloved friends, I feel almost exactly as I did earlier today along the Ashokan Way, surrounded by the refuge of my landscape. Both sanctuaries offer a grounded constancy and an undivided form of witnessing; both follow their own elegant rhythm, and both offer a safe haven from the never-ending distractions of daily life. Both the land and this Sacred Circle connect me to something larger, allowing me to release my contracted small self and return to a more expanded, compassionate self. As a fundamental element of both the natural world and this community, silence allows for a dropping down to essential truths. And in both of these refuges, beauty plays a central role—the landscape in all its mysterious glory, and the poetry, music, and artistry that make up each of our gatherings. Without these two sanctuaries I could not sustain the life I aspire to—one that is kind, creative, and fully engaged with the world. We all need some kind of safe harbor when life's storms are strong, and when we are weary. And in spite of all the busyness of our lives, we must claim our harbors and we must go to them in some sort of regular way.

APRIL

BOATING AND FISHING
CATSKILL LESSONS ON LIVING AND DYING

April 1st, the opening day of fishing season here on the Ashokan finds me thinking about a little rowboat that David and I once owned. When he and I first moved to this mountain valley, we bought the small vessel and procured a fishing license so we could explore the nooks and crannies of the reservoir that makes up our place. David named the boat *White Light,* and how we loved the vast serenity we felt on the water. Ensconced in our tiny craft out on the pristine twelve-mile reservoir, encircled by the eighteen ancients peaks that make up the Southern Catskills, we were always filled with awe and gratitude that in 1904 New York State decided to establish the Catskill Park and deemed it "forever wild." A patchwork of public and private land, the park contains forty thousand acres surrounding the Ashokan, our very own backyard, and extends out into 705,500 mountainous acres spread across four counties. How extraordinarily fortunate we all are that our forebearers had the vision to protect this open space.

Leaping fish kept us company on our outings, along with other rowboats from time to time, and abundant birdsong filled our ears. We didn't fish, but we rowed the entire shoreline, exploring a new stretch of it on each trip. The massive bluestones and enormous piles of driftwood at the water's edge became an extended outdoor sculpture garden that never ceased to captivate us, and often we would pull into one of the many enticing hidden coves to picnic or sun ourselves.

Part of the allure of the trips was seeing High Point from so many different perspectives. Each excursion brought us into a new relationship with our mountain familiar. A hollow in High Point that appeared small from the vantage point of our home, for instance, would be gigantic as we rowed our boat into an alcove right next to the base of the mountain. How invigorating it was to have our perceptions turned around and upside down. We loved steering *White Light* to places where it could give us different views of our small house too, though that was largely constant in appearing like a bird's nest snuggled into the landscape on its bluestone ledge.

Sometimes as we rowed the waters of this place of many fishes, we thought about our valley's legendary anglers, like Nick Lyons, Art Flick, Ed Ostapczuk, and Joan Wulff. Both here on the Ashokan, as well as in its many streams and rivers, Catskill fishing is a celebrated art. And, for some, it is also a veritable religion whose bible is Austin M. Francis's *Catskill Rivers*. The author describes the birthplace of American fly-fishing in the hallowed trout streams of this mountain valley—idyllic waterways like the Beaverkill, Willowemoc, Neversink, Esopus, and the Schoharie. He illuminates the mystique of Catskill angling, observing that those who fish these waters often go beyond the conventional stages of catching the most fish, or the biggest, or the most difficult, to understanding the very soul of the stream. For Austin M. Francis, fishing is about merging with nature and falling into that zone beyond time. His metaphysics of angling illuminates why the more abstract our world becomes, the more we hunger to immerse ourselves in the physicality and concrete textures of the natural world. Though David and I never actually fished on our outings, we were surely metaphysical anglers, fully merging with the tangible beauty of this place, falling into that timeless mystical realm.

Of all the fabled anglers who embody the mystique of Catskill fishing, it's the iconic Joan Wulff who most intrigues me. Known as the First Lady of fly-fishing, Joan has been casting since she was a ten-year-old girl in 1937. Vying against an all-male lineup in 1951, she captured the prestigious Fisherman's Distance Award casting a fly the distance of 161 feet. Joan went on to win multiple national and international tournament casting titles, and in 2007 she was inducted into the International Game Fish Association Hall of Fame. But it isn't just the competition that draws Joan to her sport. She has often said that it's the beauty, grace, and femininity of casting that she so loves. And there's the whole aspect of catch and release fishing that I never considered until I heard about Joan. "You can touch another living creature and feel its heartbeat," she explained in an interview. "You feel its life source, and still you release it and let it be free again. The idea of connecting with the life force of another creature without hurting it, it's just wonderful."

As the most famous woman fly fisherwoman on the planet, Joan has written many seminal books on the sport of fishing and she is also highly regarded for her passionate commitment to conservation. Through the promotion of such measures as catch and release, Joan has helped the sport of fishing to be accepted as environmentally sustainable. After marrying the late Lee Wulff, they started The Wulff School of Fly Fishing on one-hundred pristine acres in the Upper Beaverkill Valley of the Catskills. There at her school in the birthplace of American fly-fishing, Joan continues to teach the next generation of Catskill anglers about not only fish and fishing, but also about the conservation of the resource. Keeping the streams unpolluted and making sure the water and the fish remain healthy is of the utmost importance to her. "You are in beautiful places and you are there because these fish only live in clean water." Joan's words are clear, deep, and vital, like the streams she has done so much to protect.

About ten years after David and I started our reservoir outings, spring floods washed away our little rowboat. And though
we kept saying that we would replace it, our lives were busy and
we finally realized that this particular chapter of exploring our
place had come to an end. But from the very first days of living
here, both the fishing and the boating on the Ashokan have continued to enamor me, connecting me to the ancient mythology
of watercraft that I suspect the Catskill's very own soulful Austin
M. Francis and Joan Wulff also understood.

Across time and traditions, boats have been vessels of dis-
covery and initiation. In ancient Egypt, a ferry enabled the sun's
journey across the sky and escorted the souls of the dead to
the other world. So important was this craft that small models
of boats were included in every Egyptian tomb. Sacred Hindu
chants are replete with images of souls being ferried across water
to the shores of reincarnation, and in many esoteric traditions,
the boat symbolizes knowledge beyond death. In Japanese myth,
God flew down from the other side riding on a heavenly boat
made of stone, and boats of all kinds were seen as floating bridges
to heaven. Chinese mythology describes the souls of the dead as
traveling with the boat of the waning moon to "Black Moon Island," from where rebirth was possible, like the new moon coming out of darkness.

As for my own myth, I have always responded to the metaphor of life as a large body of water. In this metaphor, each individual is a small boat, and each of us the captain of our own
destiny. The waters can be calm or stormy, the skies sunny or
grey. The skillful captain navigates the storms well and gathers
strength in the good times. Other captains are afraid of danger
and lose their way, and still others don't direct their boats at all.
Regardless of the kind of captain we are, our boat continues on its
way through turbulent and peaceful times until it reaches the far

shore of death, where we cross over to the world of spirit. Rabindranath Tagore describes this crossing in the final verse of his poem, "Ocean of Forms."

> *I dive down into the depth of the ocean of forms,*
> *hoping to gain the perfect pearl of the formless.*
> *No more sailing from harbor to harbor with this my weather-beaten boat.*
> *The days are long past when my sport was to be tossed on waves.*
> *And now I am eager to die into the deathless.*

How I long to be ready to die into the deathless. At night here on the Ashokan when the fishermen hang their lanterns from the bow, the boats appear like flames floating across the dark water. I hope that when it is my time to reach the far shore, my boat will be like a bright flame floating across the water arriving at the land of spirit. I have made it known that I want my ashes thrown into the Ashokan and, perhaps, if I am fortunate, my boat will be a floating bridge to heaven.

And maybe, in its pure essence, death is similar to a new perspective, like the kind achieved when we rowed *White Light* out onto the reservoir and experienced our familiar landscape in a completely different way, though it was actually just another aspect of the same larger whole. Or perhaps death is a form of metaphysical angling, where we merge with something larger than ourselves, a realm beyond time and space. Whatever death is, I hope that if I have been a good captain of my own boat, or an attentive student of angling who has gone beyond the conventional striving for most or biggest to better understand my soul's purpose, then I will be more ready to die.

WINGED GUARDIANS OF THE INVISIBLE

After a long hard rain, thick white mists have settled in the valleys. The mists have huddled in the hollows of these mountains all morning, but now as I watch, bright shafts of light pour down from the skies and, as if by sleight of hand, appear to lift the fog. Moments later, a flock of geese lift off the reservoir in perfect V formation, honking and disappearing into those channels of light. Soon there is no trace of their flight.

I yearn to fly with those strong elegant birds, high up into the wide-open sky, the home of the invisible. Here today with the landscape's soft silence, illuminated mists, and birds with their traceless flight, I find myself pondering all that cannot be seen. Air, silence, space, sound, time, wind, presence, prayer, and the divine come to mind. I cannot see the geese's ineffable honking or the path their sturdy wings have left in the sky, but I know they exist. And I wonder: What are the essential gifts that the invisible is just waiting to offer us?

Watching birds is such a graceful bridge into the unseen. At one moment the winged creatures are down here firmly on the earth with me and then suddenly they have taken off into the sweeping azure sky, crossing over into another realm. Out on the Ashokan's vast mudflats, plovers, dunlins, and yellowlegs are all part of this bird community, along with the scoters, loons, and grebes on the water. Those who hunt in wide, open spaces—eagles, osprey, hawks, and falcons—call this place home, too. The reservoir's wide diversity of habitat—deep water, secluded coves, tundra-like flats, and thick evergreen and hardwood forest—has made the Ashokan a paradise for the winged ones. And in so many important ways, they have become my teachers.

Observing a gathering of plovers out on the mudflats, I am struck by the intense nowness of their existence. Still and erect, they sit for hours imbibing the quiet, until something startles them and they take flight—their melodious whistling calls going with them. Like the mountains, these birds are utterly themselves. I can't help but feel that this capacity to live in the now is intrinsically connected to their easy entrance into the invisible. And in their friendship with silence, space, air, and wind, all winged creatures constantly demonstrate their kinship with the imperceptible.

I have come to realize that my own interior life can't even exist unless I, too, am in intimate contact with the invisible. Silence, solitude, open space, meditation, and prayer are the fundamentals of my interior life and none are visible to my human eyes. An ongoing bond with the unseen is essential to both my faith and my capacity to find hope in a dense and complex world. But our modern addiction to all that is concrete and visible undervalues these indispensable invisible elements, and I sometimes fear that these foundations to my sanity have become endangered species. So many of us living in the prosperous Global North starve our interior lives as we stuff ourselves with more, bigger, and faster things and lifestyles. Yet all the while the landscape and the creatures patiently await us, ready to offer the essential gifts of the unseen: presence, space, silence, and the sacred. All the while the birds are the winged guardians of the precious, imperiled realm of the invisible.

I leave the plovers out on the Ashokan mudflats. It's a day for birds, and further on I sight the bald eagle majestically perched in his favorite spot atop the tallest standing pine. The eagle can rest here, motionless for many hours, complete oneness with the silence, solitude, and space being innate to his regal nature. It's even warmer now, and the low fog continues to rise up sound-

lessly into the treetops. The unexpected beauty of the giant evergreen filled with the soft white mists making their way toward
the stark white head of the eagle takes my breath away. All the
particular elements of this loveliness are visible to my eyes. But
the overall emotional impact, what transpires inside me and what
I carry away with me as I witness this beauty, is utterly invisible.

LANDSCAPE AND WRITING
AS SPIRITUAL PRACTICE

B irds of every stripe, ordinary and regal—robins, crows, hawks, and eagles—all bustle about readying their nests. Blanketed in springtime buds, the mountains appear to be clothed in mauve velvet against the sapphire sky. The valley's rosy haze is reflected in the reservoir as a rich watermelon hue. Meanwhile, multitudes of tiny blossoms burst like emerald fireworks, rendering these hardwood forests softer. It's as if the landscape is a book written in blushing pinks and chartreuse greens. Indeed, both books and the land are on my mind.

For the past three days, I have been immersed in my hometown's Woodstock Writer's Festival. This valley that is a sanctuary to countless painters and musicians, is also home to a vibrant community of writers including the likes of Gail Goodwin, Abigail Thomas, and Ed Sanders. The Writer's Festival has become an annual highlight for me, and this year the event has me thinking about writing as a way of knowing place. It has also helped me understand the striking parallels between the capacities developed by writing and those developed by time spent with the landscape. How had I failed to notice that two of my greatest loves are remarkably similar spiritual practices? At the festival, I heard André Dubus III describe how characters in his novels are sometimes more real to him than the actual people in his life. The craft of writing is a penetrating vehicle for knowing and understanding, Dubus told those of us present. When I heard that, a coup de foudre struck me as I grasped how intimate I was becoming with my landscape by writing about it. The mountains, sky, water, forests, and creatures have become, for me, like the characters in André Dubus's books become for him. The more time I spend writing about these elements, the richer and more unexpected their identities are.

I also came to see that the steadiness of the attention required in writing is similar to the steady presence of the mountains, water, or creatures. The capacity to exist in the now, which I am observing as more and more intrinsic to the land, is also a requirement of writing well. When an aspect of the natural world helps me focus and clear my mind, it's good practice for writing. In these ways, the landscape both models presence and strengthens my capacity for mindfulness as a writer.

When I sit down to write I am often tense, distracted by the myriad details and stresses of my life. But the more hours I spend focusing on the words in front of me, the more everything else falls away, and I find myself entering a realm beyond the daily demands of life. The cycle of exiled self, return to consciousness, and belonging has resurfaced in another form.

There's another striking parallel between these two essential practices of mine. The land reveals, as writing so clearly does, that truth is purely a matter of perception. This valley can simultaneously uncover the deepest sadness for one person while giving rise to unfettered joy for another. While the presence of these mountains may put one individual in touch with their feelings of deeply buried grief, for instance, his or her companion might be feeling a sense of rebirth. I experienced this mutability of truth while writing *Returning to My Mother's House,* a memoir about my mother's early death and my long-denied grief. When I sent the almost-finished manuscript to my brother and sister, their responses astonished me. My book described the sadness and loss of self I perceived in my mother's life, and my experience of her unfulfilled dreams. But my sister mostly recalled the underlying current of mom's seething anger, while my brother remembered our mother as the happiest person he had ever known. You could not have uncovered three more radically opposing views of the same mother. And all of our perspectives were true. Isabel Allende has famously said, "All of my writing is based on the premise of the mutability of fact, the mutability of memory. That it is difficult to separate fact and imagination—the lines are very blurry."

Allende could easily have been speaking about the land. How often as I walk the Ashokan Way have fact and imagination become impossibly intertwined—the way a snow squall sends me into a sandstorm in the Sahara, for instance, or the mountains, ice, water, and rocks become a majestic archetypal woman, or the mist, the wind, and the light became landscape illusionists performing sleight of hand with the visible and invisible. Both writing and the natural world encourage, perhaps even demand, that I develop fluency in moving between the material and the mystical. Time and space are mutable when I write, and they seem to be mutable for this valley that holds the past, present, and future as interchangeable parts, as well.

This cultivation of the imagination is at the very heart of what both the land and writing teach me: Go through the veil of your surface awareness. Beyond that veil, there is more to discover than you could have ever hoped. My late colleague, the poet and mystic John O'Donohue, called God the Divine Imagination. Writing and landscape are my gateways into the Divine Imagination. Said another way, these two spiritual practices inform, challenge, and change me like nothing else. I have no idea why it wasn't until now that I saw all the obvious connections between these two great loves of my life. But standing here in my landscape suffused by springtime's rosy glow, knowing that I will soon be writing about this, I experience what the Chinese call a blessing of double happiness.

MAY

ANTONIO VIVALDI
VISITS THE ASHOKAN

I t's the first of May—May Day—and chartreuse buds burst
into the cerulean sky. The bright yellow-green buds remind
me of the green ribbons my friends and I used to wind around
a Maypole when we were children. The holiday seems to pass
largely unnoticed here now, but this is not true in Ireland where
it is called Beltane, and where people decorate their front doors
with golden flowers, and the bonfires that illuminate the nighttime landscape are deemed to have protective powers. It's said
that the dew of Beltane can bring beauty, keeping you young, and
I almost put my aging face in the dewy grass along these shores.
Today there is nowhere in the world that I would rather be than
right here, walking along the Ashokan with the waves gently
breaking on rocks and the ancient Catskill range reflected in the
waters. Intoxicated by the day's loveliness, I start to hear music
as clearly as if I were sitting in the Maverick Concert hall located
just a few miles from here. I listen more carefully. Of course!
My mind is hearing Vivaldi's *Four Seasons*, with the *Allegro of Spring*
just warming up. I follow the familiar notes just as I follow the
soft hues of the familiar unfurling forest: dusty pink, coral, ochre,
mustard, mocha, soft grey, lime, and lavender. There is the Largo
in the lapping waves, the Allegro in the chorus of birdsong. Is
the land playing music, or is the music playing the land? I have
always loved this zen conundrum.

And then I remember. Last year on May Day I was in Paris, where I went to La Sainte Chapelle to hear Vivaldi's *Four Seasons*. It was an unforgettable evening in my favorite city, sitting in one of the loveliest chapels in the world. Played by the Classik Ensemble, Vivaldi's masterpiece was rendered stirring, sexy, and utterly new, as if I'd never heard the familiar piece before. The musicians played the four movements with a fierce physicality that I had never witnessed, even as a string quartet aficionado. So modern was their interpretation that I felt Vivaldi must be either cheering or turning over in his grave. I, myself, was ecstatic. David Braccini, the ensemble's director and lead violinist, read each of the sonnets that accompany the four seasonal movements, saying that the author was unknown but many believe it was Vivaldi himself.

Surely Vivaldi's sonnet for spring could have been written for this very day here on the Ashokan Way.

Spring

Allegro: Springtime is upon us. The birds celebrate her return with festive song, and murmuring streams are softly caressed by the breezes. Thunderstorms, those heralds of Spring, roar, casting their dark mantel over heaven, then die away to silence, the birds take up their charming songs once more.

Largo: On the flower—strewn meadow, with leafy branches rustling overhead, the goat-herd sleeps, his faithful dog beside him.

Allegro: Led by the festive sound of rustic bagpipes, nymphs and shepherds lightly dance beneath the brilliant canopy of spring.

Surrounded by birdsong and breezes, I hear the final Allegro starting up. Now I, too, can see the nymphs dancing out on the reservoir's sparkling waters. And there are the shepherds making their way down this mountain range. And beneath this forest's canopy of spring I can almost see Antonio Vivaldi himself. Come, I want to say, walk with me along the shores of this place of many fishes. Gaze upon these waters that are home to such a rare diversity of winged creatures, these ancient bluestone mountains whose walk is so constant. Open your ears to this precious open space that offers its music with such free abandon. Do you hear how this landscape is playing your sonnet for spring?

When I get home I put on Classik Ensemble's recording of Vivaldi's masterpiece. Facing out toward the Ashokan Way, I lie on the couch with my eyes closed as the *Four Seasons* pour over me. I am filled with the perfect counterpart to what I have just experienced. Now the music evokes my landscape, just as vividly as the land had just evoked Vivaldi's music. Lying in my living room as the allegro of "Winter" comes on, I am in a snowstorm with the entire valley a dazzling white; "Spring's" allegro imbues my being with the birth of red buds and chirping baby birds; with "Summer's" largo I am walking along the reservoir on a languid day with the fish jumping; and now with each note of "Autumn's" allegro, my mountains burst with another fall color.

I have that mysterious feeling when one thing has so become like the other that I no longer know where one begins and the other ends. On this May Day, the land played Vivaldi's music, and his music brought the landscape inside to me. Inside becoming outside, and outside becoming inside. We are all wound together like the streamers in a Maypole: Allegro, largo, and allegro winding around winter, spring, summer, and fall; birdsong, breeze, mountains, nymphs, and shepherds winding around me.

Heaven Here On Earth
Reconciliation of Opposites

Behold another splendid day as the mural of spring spreads out right before my eyes. The multiple subtle shades of green are dizzying, climbing their way up the mountains like a multi-colored staircase as they replace the mauve of red buds. At the junctures where the red bleeds into the green, the ridges appear indigo, sharply-defined lines suggesting deep crevices. All week I have been green drunk, intoxicated by the sensual colors and birdsong bursting from the trees. The rare dogwood appears as delicate white lace woven into the vast emerald forest. It's been a long time since we have had such a string of stunning days, like heaven come down to earth. This makes me ponder how I can conduct my life as if heaven were indeed here on earth.

Oh, how the personality of these mountains changes in the spring! In the winter, the Catskills appear distant and detached, bedecked in their formal white attire. But now they appear closer and more intimate. Exuberant in gowns of chartreuse silk and yellow brocade, these peaks appear ready to go dancing right across the cornflower blue sky. The mountains and I, we are both green drunk! I see that it's not just the mountains whose personality changes with the seasons. I, too, undergo a shift when spring arrives. Leaving behind my quieter, more internally focused rhythms until next winter, I become more extroverted. The Woodstock astronomer and author Bob Berman writes about how the sky, too, undergoes a radical personality transformation in the month of May.

"The brilliant but heavy-handed winter constellations now plummet into the west, consumed by the crepuscular fires of dusk. The giant planet Jupiter is sinking lower each evening. With the sunsets getting later, and the stars marching eternally into the west, it was forever destined that the two opposing armies—twilight and winter stars —would meet headlong each spring."

While the night skies are in their darkest dormancy in the spring, the earth is bursting with vitality and color. This cosmic juxtaposition strikes me as the perfect unification of opposites. Perhaps it is this planetary changing of the guard that leaves me feeling like heaven is now on the ground where I walk.

Another of this season's iconic symbols announces itself as I come upon a family of geese with four tiny goslings tucked around their mama's ample sides. Fluffy balls of mustard-and-mocha-colored feathers, the babies are sunning themselves on this fine day. As I pass by, the papa goose hisses loudly and protectively. On my return, the little family is just entering the water, and as I watch, the goslings' impossibly tiny webbed feet begin to kick as they glide into the reservoir. The water is calm today and I am relieved for these creatures small enough to fit into the palm of my hand. The mother and father float languidly, but keep an eye on their offspring.

Earlier this week, though, I watched as another family of geese entered these waters on a day so rough that the turbulent waves tossed the babies mercilessly. Mesmerized, I stood by helplessly as the family with five little ones left behind a gosling when he couldn't keep up. The tiny ball of fluff struggled mightily, heaved up and down by the powerful current. All I could do was shout at the geese, imploring them to wait. But drown the gosling did, and I was left to ponder.

When the composed rhythm of the natural world calms and steadies me, it's a balm to my soul. But nature's dispassionate stance can be utterly terrifying. I will never forget my walks along the Ashokan Way after Hurricane Irene devastated the Hudson Valley in August of 2011. I found myself dazed by the sheer scale of the storm's massive path of destruction. Thousands of toppled trees lay in these woods like dead soldiers on a battlefield, their giant roots reaching up to heaven in a last desperate gesture. With wide swathes of felled trees cut into the forest, my familiar skyline vanished and a strange, wounded one took its place. The sky itself, in the immediate aftermath of the storm, was an eerie tarnished-pewter color; the air smelled burnt. For months following the hurricane the reservoir remained the color of dried blood, with immense carcasses of wood—trunks and massive limbs—floating on the surface. Out on the mudflats, flocks of displaced birds landed like refugees from a war zone.

For days washouts created rushing rivers along our roads and power lines lay downed at every turn, leaving thousands without power for long periods of time; our generator ran for twelve days. At the height of the flooding our neighbors were forced to abandon their car and walk home in knee-deep water, while other friends living directly on the Rondout creek evacuated their home carrying their most precious belongings, fearing they would never return. Hurricane Irene rendered everything—earth, sky, water, forests, creatures, and humans—helpless. This force of nature paraded her celebrated indifference.

Yes, nature can cure, and it can also be brutally destructive. As a master teacher of paradox, the earth is clearly trying to show me that I cannot have one without the other. These mountains are both distant and intimate; the sky is bright in the dark of winter and somber in the light of spring; the reservoir is calm and comforting as well as rough and unforgiving; the geese are both protective of and merciless to their offspring; this valley's storms can bring replenishing rains and terrifying devastation; and all year the seasons are dying and then being reborn.

And I, too, am compassionate and cruel, nurturing and destructive, warm and cold, light and dark. I, too, am dying and being reborn throughout my seasons. At every turn since my youth in the Brandywine River Valley, the natural world has been patiently teaching me about the reconciliation of opposites, but I think it is only now, after a lifetime of paying close attention to the landscape, that I am finally beginning to grasp the lesson it has been offering me. I am finally able to understand that only by living between the opposites that naturally exist in the world, by respecting and learning equally from both sides, will I be able to find a state of true equanimity. It is when I neither cling to the part of the opposite I desire nor push away the part I fear that I conduct my life as if heaven were right here on earth.

MOTHER MARY
IN THE PLACE OF MANY FISHES

A pale, robin's egg blue sky invites me into my morning walk on this soft spring day just before the full moon of May, the flower moon. Mists are rising off the mountains like a veil lifting to reveal a face. The Catskills are fully garbed in greenery now, and their reflection in the reservoir is a mellow chartreuse hue. Over the Ashokan a great blue heron offers its unique croaking call as it flaps its way east; geese headed west echo with their own version of honking. Choirs of birdsong waft through the emerald forest. Everything feels soft, as if the sky, the mountains, the trees, the birds, and the water are wrapping me in their tender embrace.

This softness of this season is such a stark contrast to my internal state during this, my busiest time of year. With their endless details, lists of people to contact, projects to supervise, and money to raise, these weeks leave me feeling tense and contracted. I brace myself against the day, my body stiffened with painful knots of stress. There are moments when all these pressures can leave me hating my life. But just now I can hear the landscape's expansive voices say, "Come rest inside this sanctuary of open space, let us hold you and calm you. Let us smooth away your hard edges and soften your heart again." The kindness of their offering brings me to tears, and I feel the truth of John Muir's words: "Nature in her green tranquil woods heals and soothes all afflictions."

No matter where in the world I find myself, I have always prayed the Hail Mary as I walk. Today I pray for surrender, and for the ability to find space in my crowded, stressed life. Hail

Mary full of grace, I say as I slide my fingers across my well-worn rosary beads. How I love saying the rosary here along the Ashokan shores. As I recite each round of the prayer to Mary, my hands move along the beads and my feet step in rhythm to the familiar words. Over the years Mother Mary and the Ashokan have become like close sisters to me, each of them a facet of the sacred. And it pleases me to imagine the Mother Mary here, in this place of many fishes. Now I can distinctly feel my own prayers joining with the benedictions of this land. I experience Mary's nurturing presence as identical to the landscape's tender embrace. As I surrender, all around me I have a sensation of what I can only call grace. The sky, the mountains, the forests, and the water appear illuminated, unified, as if they were breathing together. I can feel these elements breathing restoration and space into me and through me. As tears come, I stop by the water's edge, allowing this breath to heal me. I don't know how long I sit, but when I rise to leave I am soft with the space of the universe inside me.

Clothed in this garb of spaciousness, I return to my office. Although the details of my urgent to-do lists threaten to bury me, the landscape's steady presence continues to hold me. Still breathing inside me, the land reminds me that in a few months all these pressing details, the ones I am so worked up over, will have vanished forever. There will be little trace of them left. But the sky, the mountains, the trees, and the water will still be here waiting to offer me something more lasting, something more essential. A line from one of my favorite writers of place, Terry Tempest Williams, floods my being. As if she were here in the room conversing with me, she says: "We have forgotten what we can count on. The natural world provides refuge. Each of us harbors a homeland, a landscape we naturally comprehend." And I reply that at the same time, each landscape harbors certain people they naturally comprehend.

SUMMER

JUNE

ONE DESIGN OF THE MOVING
AND VIVACIOUS MANY

Days of stifling humidity have been followed by torrential rain, wind, and bone-chilling cold, but now we are given this day from the gods. As a breeze wafts off the Ashokan, the light is so pure that I feel I can see every undulation along these ancient bluestone ridges, every shade of green in the forest. The tall grass appears illuminated from within. "*La lumiere des fees*," or fairy light, is the perfect description for this luminance. Spring is in her old age, fully aware that in just a few days she will fade away into summer. But for now, this sensuous season is breathtaking in all her mature glory.

Fish leap, tiny fawns stay close to their mothers, and those vulnerable goslings I was so worried about just weeks ago are now honking ugly ducklings waddling confidently away from their parents. Growing by leaps and bounds, the baby eagles flap their wings, practicing for first flight. The regal blue heron lands on her favorite outcropping of stone while a red-tailed hawk traces lazy circles in the azure sky. Birdsong has reached its crescendo, and the exuberant chorus leaves me wanting to know more about particular birdcalls in the same way that I love to follow the individual instruments in string quartets. Having recently reread John Burroughs' *In The Catskills*, I find myself envying the famous naturalist's profound knowledge of birds. Burroughs could immediately recognize the songs and calls of rare species, and here he describes the Bicknell's thrush as if he were describing a cello or a violin: " The song is a minor key, finer, more attenuated, and

more under the breath than that of any other thrush. It seemed as
if the bird was blowing in a delicate, slender, golden tube, so fine
and yet so flute-like and resonant the song appeared ... it was but
the soft hum of the balsams, interpreted and embodied in a bird's
voice." At this moment there is nothing I long for more than to
hear a Bicknell's thrush.

I walk on through the chartreuse explosion of the fern forest fully unfurled against the lush backdrop of bushy long-needle
pines. So vibrant is this woodland of yellow-green and evergreen
that it offers up a palpable infusion of vitality. When the wind
stirs, the thick sweet scent of clover pours over me. The monarchs dip ecstatic into the source of this fragrance, their yellow
wings fluttering among the dense pink hedges. My gaze lowers
just as a painted turtle, dressed in its shiny black shell with delicate red patterns, lumbers across my path. It's an auspicious sign
since it's rare to catch sight of a turtle here on the reservoir. And
today I see that my favorite enchanted creatures have returned
to these Ashokan shores—the dragonflies with their translucent
burgundy wings.

Just as I am feeling that this day could not get more lovely,
a stand of wild yellow irises at the foot of the eagles' peninsula
stops me dead in my tracks. Its beauty is so singular and so tran-
sient that I lose all sense of time and space. As I fall into that
unnamable place where those wild yellow irises were created, I
know that this landscape holds countless miracles just waiting to
reshape me. I know that my rational mind doesn't stand a chance
up against all this beauty and mystery. And for this I am grateful
beyond measure. I remember Mary Oliver's entreaty, "...that your
spirit grow in curiosity, that your life be richer than it is, that you
bow to the earth as you feel how it actually is, that we—so clever,
and ambitious, and selfish, and unrestrained—are only one design of the moving, the vivacious many."

By now I have imbibed so much wonder that I am completely intoxicated. I cannot help but offer my unabashedly drunken song to this place. Oh, wild yellow iris, red-tattooed turtle, shimmering burgundy dragonflies, and fluttering monarchs. Oh, unfurled chartreuse fern forests and lush long-needle pines, *lumiere des fees* and ancient bluestone ridges. Oh, Bicknell's thrush, red-tailed hawk, regal blue heron, flapping baby eagles, and honking ugly ducklings. If I know one thing, it is that I am only one design of your moving, vivacious many.

THE MOUNTAINS AND MASTER DŌGEN
THREE TEACHINGS

The vivid light refracts in so many directions that the valley seems to wear a necklace of shimmering quartz crystals this morning. The crescent moon hangs in the sapphire sky like a jaunty cap flung into the cosmos. And, continuing with wardrobe metaphors, I see that these mountains have changed into their summer garb. Wearing a full skirt of diaphanous gauzy green, they are cool and ready for the season's heat. This Catskill skirt is the sort you twirl in, kicking up your bare feet. How different this valley in its sheer summer dancing skirt feels to me compared to when it wears spring's heavy robes fully laden with dense blossoms, or winter's formal icy white gowns. With every season these mountains have endless wisdom to offer me.

One of the ways I have begun to more fully understand all that this mountain valley has to teach me is through Master Dōgen's magnificent work, *The Mountains and Rivers Sutra*. I have been rereading Carl Bielefeldt's translation of this teaching Sutra, which was first introduced to me by the late John Daido Loori, former Abbott of the Zen Mountain Monastery located fifteen minutes from where I now stand. The Mountains and Rivers Sutra had a profound impact on Daido Loori and his vision for what would become one of the leading Zen monasteries in the West. In this Sutra, Dōgen writes that the mountains contain everything we need to know. And on this radiant June day, I am reflecting particularly on three teachings that Master Dōgen has helped me to appreciate.

"These mountains and rivers of the present are the actualization of the word of the ancient Buddhas. ...Because
they are the state prior to the kalpa of emptiness, they are
living in the present. Because they are the self before the
germination of any subtle sign, they are liberated in their
actualization."

All day long the ancient bluestone peaks surrounding me are
simply, and profoundly, being themselves. They exist in the present, and in this state they offer their most penetrating teaching.
I so yearn to absorb this lesson from my mountain valley, and on
some days I can inhabit their generous wisdom. Most the time
though, I am not fully present in the now, but far away belabor-
ing the past or frantically planning the future. But I am learning that devoted attention is a worthy gateway into the present.
When I am truly mindful of this landscape with its sky and water,
forests and creatures, I am instantly in the present. Here along
the Ashokan Way, my attention is both softly receptive but also
sharply focused. With its incomparable patience the land has
shown me that I cannot hunt down the present, but must quietly
wait for what draws me into the moment. And if I come here every day expecting to see something new, I am sure to strengthen
my capacity to live in the now.

"The mountains, unchanged in body and mind, maintaining their own mountain countenance, have always been
traveling about studying themselves."

Like many of the teachings of Master Dogen, this one sentence is so dense with wisdom that it becomes a full Dharma talk,
a vital discourse on how to live. The mountains are utterly themselves, and every day they encourage me to find my own countenance. My very own countenance—not that of my parents or

my husband, or my peers or my colleagues, and not that of the famous people I admire. Maintaining their natural character, the mountains travel about studying themselves. If I can find my own true identity and then journey to understand and fulfill my calling, I will have lived well. Of all the gifts that these Catskill Mountains have given me, their constancy is among the most precious. Unchanged, they have always been traveling to remain true to themselves in both body and mind. This has taught me to be faithful to the physical and mental practices that strengthen my own character. And to keep these practices simple. How instructive that constancy is the close sister of devotion. Elegant and sustainable, there is absolutely no waste or distraction in this path of maintaining my own countenance. This is the way—constant, simple, and sustainable—that I long to live. This is why the ancients felt that we could most clearly understand the deep structure of things when in the presence of a mountain landscape.

> "There is a mountain walk and a mountain flow. Because the blue mountains are walking, they are constant. Their walk is swifter than the wind."

Here Master Dōgen illuminates the constant tension of opposites inherent in living here on the earth's dualistic plane. Everything has both sides. Nothing is simply what it appears to be. Some days when I walk among them, these mountains are all solid rock, anchored down here on earth. But other days they flow like a giant river, moving over me in waves. I, too, am solid rock and flowing water, rational and emotional, stable and everchanging. My steadiness enables my fluidity; my constancy allows me to be swifter than the wind. We cannot contain any one side without also living the other side. This sounds so simple but all of us human creatures struggle to honor the contradictions that live inside us as well as in those we love, and to respect the opposites embedded in every aspect of the world we inhabit. But all day long the landscape is demonstrating how to do this. This is why I come to these mountains: The most constant presence that I know, they are simultaneously and utterly different each time I encounter them. Their walk, their endless capacity to inform me, is indeed swifter than the wind—illusive, pervasive, and frequently wildly unexpected. It is they who tell me the truth, they who patiently advise me how to live.

DHARMA AS TRUE NATURE
STRAWBERRY MOON, EXTENDED TWILIGHT, AND TEJASWI

On this languid summer evening, David and I are walking near the time of sunset. Everything is slow and quiet in the heat; a deer rests in a field of clover and the blue heron is still as a statue. The fish seem to flop rather than leap, and even the flapping of the baby eagles' wings seem half-hearted. Enticed by the pungent fragrance of clover hedges, we stop along the Ashokan shores to watch the sun go down. As the fiery ball slips behind the peaks, Highpoint, South, Table, Lone, Rocky, and Balsam turn a rich slate blue, earning their name: the Blue Mountains. Swathes of peach and mauve flood the sundown sky as night crickets begin their song. We are just past the summer solstice, and these longest days of light also give way to the longest twilight. And tonight's full moon, the strawberry moon, is the largest of the year.

Awaiting the moonrise in this extended twilight, I am reflecting on the day we have just spent with our remarkable colleague Tejaswi Sevekari, whose home is in Pune, India. For all of her adulthood Teju, as we fondly call her, has worked with her NGO Saheli to serve disenfranchised women sold into sex trafficking. Over the course of the years we have worked with her, Tejaswi has inspired us with her dedication, her humility, and her dry humor. Today she, David, and I have plotted the strategy for our ongoing partnership in India.

Our collaboration with Tejaswi represents the embodiment of my deepest passion: bringing agency and consciousness to the disenfranchised. All my work over the past thirty-six years has led to this chapter, as if my dharma, or life calling, has finally come to its fullest fruition. And Teju's life has taught me so much about how to fully embody one's dharma. Today she discussed with us her observation that for the women with whom she works, the beginning of agency, or the development of inner resources that catalyze desired actions, takes place during an introspective dialogue when they ask themselves whether they will succumb to their victimhood or not. At the moment they take responsibility for transforming their victimization, consciousness is born. Ultimately, Teju concluded, while sex workers, those abused and disenfranchised, and other people living in poverty didn't create their circumstances, they have to be the primary agents in changing those circumstances not only for themselves, but for their families and their societies. To help them do so, Saheli, Teju's NGO, has organized the sex workers in Pune into a collective in order amplify their voices, and Tejaswi herself is working toward her doctoral degree focused on the power of collectives to effect social change.

Over these past few years, Tejaswi has been my teacher in more ways than she knows. She has described in graphic detail how girls as young as ten-years-old are sold as sex slaves. They service men in tiny stalls with filthy mats on the ground. Many of them spend their entire lives in the brothels and many suffer from AIDS. But that is not what we must focus on, she has clearly and repeatedly told me in her lilting Indian accent. "What is important is how to build their agency. What is important is how much dignity and resiliency these women have, how they also have dreams for their lives just like we all do. Please don't feel sorry for my women," Teju tells me. "Think about them with respect and assume that they are just as smart, if not more so, than you are. They come up with ideas and solutions to their challenges that you could never imagine."

Teju has also taught me not to judge the parents who sell their daughters into brothels since I cannot possibly comprehend a level of poverty where I would be forced to choose between being able to feed six children if I sell one daughter, or having them all starve if I don't sell that child. Because the women themselves are able to understand this, some of the sex workers go back to their villages and forgive their parents. Tejaswi herself role models this non judgmental stance as she has started to work in collaborative ways with the archenemy of her sex workers, the brothel keepers. She believes that lasting positive change will come to the sex-trafficking sector only when all parties work together. When I am with Tejaswi I have a palpable sensation of a person deliberately and fully living her dharma. And so abundant is Teju's ownership of her soul's work that it spills over, fortifying me.

On a recent trip to Jordan I was in a tiny room packed with Syrian refugees, some wearing bright red and purple headscarves, and others dressed all in black and so heavily veiled I could just make out their eyes. Through my translator, I understood that the women wanted to hear about my life, but I found myself uncharacteristically shy and tongue-tied. And then I heard Teju's clear voice in my head: "Treat every person you meet with respect and assume they are smarter than you are." With Tejaswi's words guiding me, I told the refugees something about my life, my institute, and my lingering doubts that I have the knowledge and strength required to sustain my work. When I finished they had so much to say to me that my translator could barely keep up. In animated Arabic, they suggested that I ask for more help from the women I work with on the ground in Africa, India, and the Middle East. " You are too isolated," the Syrian women told me. "And you're not supposed to have all the answers. " They didn't have to say out loud that if they could live with hope, what reason on earth could I possibly give for my own challenges? During this entire visit I felt Teju at my side, smiling.

Tejaswi's spirit has accompanied me at other times, too, when I have been with people dying of AIDS, or genocide survivors who have lost entire families, or women in war zones who have been repeatedly gang raped. The more of the world I am exposed to, the more astounded I am by the resilience of the human spirit. I wonder if, under such circumstances, I could carry myself with the kind of dignity that I have witnessed in so many others. And the more I understand about our world, the more I understand that any injustice anywhere endangers justice everywhere; and that our liberation must be mutual, brought about by reciprocity, collaboration, and a radical equality.

Coming back to this moment on the shores of the Ashokan with David, my partner in this work since its very inception, I am pondering all that this landscape has taught me about agency and consciousness, and about the fulfillment of dharma that comes from being true to one self. This mountain valley has always encouraged me toward the kind of introspection that Teju spoke of as a necessary prerequisite to agency. It is here in this outer landscape that I have traveled deep inside my own territory, facing my hidden fears and my own places of victimization. With its incomparable ability to be itself, the land is constantly inspiring me to be myself, to be the agent of my own destiny. It is continuously reminding me that no circumstance can take my agency away from me. When I think of dharma as living one's true nature, I see that all along these mountains and this sky, these forests and this water, have been quietly showing me how to do exactly that.

Like today's full moon, the current phase of my work is at its most expansive. And Tejaswi's spirit is like these longest days of light with their extended twilight. Her example of fully embodying her dharma—with a mind that penetrates below surface appearances, a heart that has remained open in spite of the tremendous suffering she has encountered, and humor and hope in the face of the harshest realities—casts a light that is long and lasting. And now the strawberry moon rises up round, robust, and rosy. As this largest moon of the year spreads out inside me, I feel the fullness of our shared human consciousness residing in me. And all that Teju has taught me now joins this moonlight, sparkling across the water with its silvery incandescence.

JULY

CROWS

WHEN THE ORDINARY BECOMES EXTRAORDINARY

I have started my walk early but already it's hot and humid. Everything coated in the heat's dense haze, even the mountains' reflection in the reservoir, appears glazed over. Summer's emerald forest is utterly still.

I am moving slowly in the humidity when the caw of crows in the field below breaks into my reverie. I see, as well as hear, these birds almost every day along the Ashokan Way. In the winter, their shimmering black coats are vivid against the white snow. When spring comes, their excited calls echo across the water as they collect long grass for their nests. On clear summer days, their plumage gives off a violet-iridescent glow. And during the autumn, their charcoal color is beautifully set off by the bright foliage. They are so ordinary though, so commonplace, that I don't really pay attention to them in the way that I pay attention to a hawk, an eagle, or a blue heron. But now their cawing is so loud it has made me curious.

Down in the field below there are myriad crows, too many to count. They cover a portion of the grassy hillside like a lustrous inky blanket. Mesmerized, I stand for long minutes watching as the birds drop sticks and grass on something. Over and over, they land and fly off, land and fly off. Eventually, their raucous chorus slows, and in the relative quiet an article I recently read on animal empathy comes flooding back into my consciousness. I learned that crows are known to surround their dead with almost ceremonial precision. Scientists posit that the birds are paying tribute to the one who has died, and even display behavior that suggests they are experiencing grief.

Realizing that I am witnessing a crow funeral, I now pay attention in a different way. The cawing becomes a funeral dirge, rising and falling in a haunting, mournful song. I see that the growing pile of sticks and grass is a deliberate and poignant offering to the dead, and that the silent sitting of the crows is a dignified prayer amplified by the power of their large community. It's hard to imagine a more honorable funeral than this. For a long time I watch, thinking about how even the ordinary is extraordinary, how too often something I know well can seem ordinary, but really that's just a signal that I have stopped paying attention.

Sometimes I think I know everything about David, my husband of thirty-six years. But the moment I bring real presence to our marriage, he is a wonderful mystery all over again. He shares a part of his childhood that I have never heard before, or an insight into a mutual friend, or a kind reflection about something that I can't see in myself—and he is new to me all over again. With dear friends, how easy it is to fall into the lazy pattern of feeling that I have already heard their stories and histories rather than recognizing that they are courageously entering the next level in their life's spiral. After all, my story remains the same, too. Like theirs, it is all too familiar, but also miraculous. With students or clients, how often I become impatient when they seem stuck or resistant for longer than I think they should be, rather than bringing the true awareness necessary to appreciate their suffering. Is any one or any creature really ordinary if we are paying close attention?

Back at home I do an online search for crow symbols and myths. Quickly I learn that these birds appear in hundreds of legends in cultures around the world, often as supernatural creatures with magical powers. They appear, in different traditions, as the principal envoys of the makers of life, Odin and Apollo; they serve or defy the wind, the lords of death, and Satan; they are featured in stories in which they bring the sun, stars, water, tides, or humans into this world. Is it really any wonder then that crows display empathy and engage in complex rituals to mourn their dead? I will treasure the memory of scores of them gathered in the green summer field, their inky black plumage shimmering as they honored their own. What a moving reminder that the rigorous practice of true presence—seeing a person with a fresh beginner's mind—is a prerequisite to love. And a reminder as well of Master Dogen's teaching that "In the mundane nothing is sacred. In sacredness, nothing is mundane."

FOUR BLACK BEARS
INTO THE LONG BODY OF THE ASHOKAN WAY

The day is ungodly hot and I have decided to walk at dusk. I've parked at the edge of the reservoir and am just about to get out of my car when my gaze lands on something I've never seen in decades of walking here: in the field below, three black bear cubs and their mother are heading across the meadow into the forest. The mama appears huge next to her little ones and I'm glad to be watching from my car, knowing how notoriously protective mother bears are of their cubs. The young bears scramble to keep up, cuffing each other, and it looks to me like they're having fun.

They are absolutely lovely as they lumber through the soft twilight. Though New York's largest concentration of black bears live right here in the Catskills, there are still only about two thousand of them. Now as I walk in this hour of transition from day to night, the four creatures usher me through a portal back into a time when the black bear roamed this land. Thousands of years before Christ, the bear followed the swollen Esopus Creek up from its mouth at the Hudson River to arrive at this place of many fishes. Though the food was abundant, the creatures would have needed to be wary, as rattlesnakes were plentiful and the Esopus people of the Wolf Clan were superb hunters. The Esopus spoke Algonkian, and as I walk along these shores this evening I am still surrounded by the echoes of their language. Tongore, Moonhaw, Peekamoose, Shandaken, Onteora, and Ashokan—names of towns, mountains, and lakes—are all derived from Algonkian.

Cadences from their language help me conjure up the native Esopus peoples who the bear had to reckon with. The land was covered with lichens, mosses, and shrubs, and the ample supply of nourishment brought mammoths and caribou to graze here in the summer. Stalking in groups, the Esopus drove their prey into the sticky traps of bogs and killed them with large javelins. Like many other hunter-gatherer peoples, they were animists who felt that all living things had spirits. Eventually the fierce spear throwers were replaced by a generation who used bows and arrows to hunt the bear and deer who roamed these forests.

Subsequent generations of the Wolf Clan lived in small extended family groups in the hills beside the Esopus, Rondout, and Wallkill creeks. While they continued to hunt the forest with bows and arrows, they also utilized every patch of available soil in the surrounding valleys for pasture or for crops of corn, beans, and tobacco. The land's abundant supply of stone provided them plenty of material with which to shape spears, arrow points, knives, drills, and scrapers, and if the black bear watched from the forest, they might see the Wolf Clan making pottery, building their round shelters with frames of saplings and covering of bark, or fashioning dugout canoes. Not only a means of transportation, these sleek boats also served the purpose of storing corn for the winter when buried in pits dug into the earth, and lined with mats woven of reed or the bark of trees. But, as the black bear knew well, above all else the Esopus people were hunters. Setting fires on the lower slopes of the Catskills, they cleared habitat in order to drive bear and deer to open land where they could better hunt them.

Respecting the elegant cyclical nature of the seasons, the Esopus understood the particular abundance of each time of year. When good runs of herring or shad came up the Hudson they went out to fish; in summer when the streams were low, they harvested water clams. In the fall entire families, including the dogs, set out for rock shelters formed on the sides of the Catskills by overhanging ledges where they hunted the bear, deer, and wild turkeys. As the men hunted into early winter when light snow made tracking game easier, the women prepared meat and made skins into clothing. While they were legendary hunters, the Esopus were also known for their reverence for all living creatures. Like most native peoples of that era, the Wolf Clan engaged in refined rituals demonstrating their respect and gratitude for the creatures they hunted. Did the black bear sense that these would be the last peoples to treat the earth and all its inhabitants as sacred?

Later in the 1700s, the habitat of both the Esopus people and the black bear would have been interrupted when the Dutch farmers, who settled in the Hudson River Valley, began to cut primitive roads along the Esopus trails. Like that of the Wolf Clan, the bears' way of life was coming to an end.

And then by the early nineteenth century, the vast silence that the black bear had known for so long was broken by the thunderous rumbling of huge wagons. They were carrying hides from South America up from the sloops along the Hudson on to tanneries in the Catskills. Hemlock planks from the tanneries and sawmills now covered the old Esopus trails, making better roads for the wagons. In the town of Ashokan, the air was filled with the swirling red dust of the hemlock bark being crushed in huge vats to tan the hides. By now, the black bear would have retreated high up into the remote mountain peaks and caves. And soon the hemlock would be gone and a turnpike built, followed by a railroad.

With that railroad came the famed bluestone quarries, where huge slabs of sandstone were cut from high up on the Catskill mountainsides. Were the black bear watching from their dens? Dragged down these mountains by oxen and loaded on the docks at the Rondout creek, the bluestone made its way south to New York City where the stone was laid to become the famous sidewalks of New York, some of which still exist. Throughout the late nineteenth and early twentieth century the people of New York City headed in the opposite direction, boarding the trains to escape the summer heat and disease and become the tourists of the Catskills.

My journey back in time closes as my walk ends. But during this twilight hour my recollection of the black bear's lineage has helped me to trace the history of this valley, and though these chapters of history are closed, they still vividly exist in my mind. The past still shapes how I view this place today and how I respond when I see four black bear lumbering across a summer field. Echoes and shadows of the old remain alongside the new. Now my footsteps and my story are also part of the long body of the Ashokan Way. And as the dusk transforms into night, I am acutely aware of how both the land and the creatures inhabiting it hold the past and present with seamless equanimity. Once again the landscape has expanded my sense of time. I see how the past is still here, and the present is deeply enriched by my connection to it.

BALD HEAD ISLAND

WHAT DO I KNOW WHEN I AM IN THIS PLACE

THAT I CAN KNOW NOWHERE ELSE?

Each summer for more than twenty-five years David and I have spent a month on a tiny barrier island off the coast of North Carolina. In contrast to our home in the mountains, Bald Head Island's landscape is utterly flat; as we look out onto the marsh's vast expanse of chartreuse spartina, the open horizon of sky spreads out before us into seemingly limitless space. We bask in the continuous company of Great American egrets and their smaller cousins, snowy egrets, along with my favorite birds of all, the heron family—great blue, Louisiana, green, and night-heron. From our dock we can see and smell the sea. The overall feeling is of light, water, and air. The stark difference between this barrier island and the Ashokan Way, with its sky full of mountains and its solid presence of earth and bluestone, has me contemplating a question posed by the superb writer of place Robert Macfarlane.

> "For some time now it has seemed to me that the two questions we should ask of any strong landscape are these: firstly, what do I know when I am in this place that I can know nowhere else? And then, vainly, what does this place know of me that I cannot know of myself?"

Sitting at the edge of Cape Fear with miles of untouched white powder beach, Bald Head Island is a protected sanctuary for egrets, herons, ibis, osprey, and loggerhead turtles. It is a protected sanctuary for us, as well. For a month we live on a tidal marsh creek, with the changing tides a visceral reminder of the natural rhythm of life. Flowing into the creek is full, and flowing out of the creek is empty. Fullness, emptiness, fullness, emptiness, the tides conduct their master class. With the primal purity of their cadence, the tides have taught us that a full life that never empties is unsustainable and without beauty. I don't believe we could have ever learned the creek's lesson in our home in a mountain valley whose solidity and constancy is what has helped shape our disciplined life of concrete manifestation.

Instead of taking a solitary daily walk on the rocky shores of the Ashokan Way, I stroll with David along miles of untouched beach with the aquamarine sea stretching out before us like the very definition of generosity. Hours of floating in the warm ocean render us empty and restored. We make a daily pilgrimage to the furthest tip of Cape Fear, Frying Pan Shoals, the setting of countless pirate legends and ghost stories. Perched at what feels like the very edge of the world, the shoals are a series of complex underwater labyrinths where the cross currents are fierce and unrestrained. Standing knee deep in the undercurrents, we offer our prayers and intentions out into this primordial place of power. Summer after summer these potent crisscrossing waters have bestowed their benediction, a visceral mandate to keep mixing up the currents of our lives. This is something I know when I am in this place that I can know nowhere else.

David and I are now in our late-sixties, and our lives have never felt more like the waters at Frying Pan Shoals. Like the complex currents at Cape Fear, our work consists of a series of unlikely intersections between our projects in the affluent Global

North and our endeavors in the developing Global South. Cross-generational currents sweep in at every turn, and the wild crossing over of diverse sectors—grassroots, corporate, government, arts, and social entrepreneurship—creates unexpected pathways. Thus a vital lesson learned on a tiny barrier island off the coast of North Carolina has traveled with us across sectors, generations, and geographies.

And what of Robert Macfarlane's second question, what does Bald Head know of me that I cannot know of myself? My small island tells me, "You are both a blue mountain and blue heron. And though it's true that you live most of your life like the mountain, you would be well served to spend more of your life like the heron in the tidal marsh creek, carefully observing the balance between fullness and emptiness."

AUGUST

THE MAVERICK SPIRIT
IN THESE MOUNTAINS AND IN ME

I am back on the Ashokan Way after our month on Bald Head Island. I arrive at *l'heure bleue,* the time between early evening and nightfall when the sky is periwinkle and the mountains are as positively blue as their name. After weeks away at the seaside, I immediately feel how dense and solid this landscape is and I have an overpowering sense of being held by the rocks and the earth of this mountain valley. How I have missed this far-reaching view down the vales and across to the peaks that rise, individual height next to individual height, until they blend like currents in a giant river. Unlike the ever-dominant sky at Bald Head, here the sky willingly serves as a mere backdrop for these solid bluestone shapes. I take back each lovely ledge, hollow, and slope as if it were a part of me from which I have been separated, and each of these familiar contours of my home landscape finds its corresponding landscape inside me. There is the hollow that reminds me of my sorrow. It is the ledge of a new challenge where I am afraid to leap off into the unknown, and the gentle slope that allows me to rest from my tendency to spend too much time in overdrive. Listening to the lapping waves against the rocky shores of the reservoir, I recall how many times this water has opened my heart, allowing my tears to flow. Here I am, spread across this valley with all of my changing aspects, soft and fluid, concrete and constant. I know with the same solidity of these ancient peaks that this is where I belong. This is where I live and work, where I have built my marriage, my home, and my community.

Happy to be home and strolling along the reservoir, I hear echoes of the hundreds of walks I have taken here, hundreds of pathways into deeper self-understanding. And right along with these echoes I hear the reverberation of the music I listened to only an hour ago at the Maverick Concert Hall, located just ten minutes from here. During the summer months, Sunday afternoon concerts at the Maverick Festival and my walks through this land go hand and hand, as I digest whatever music I've just heard by hiking the Ashokan Way. Indeed, music and landscape have always been havens of inspiration and restoration for me. And the arts have always been an intrinsic part of what shapes the character of a place. In this valley—home to Woodstock's vibrant artists' colony of musicians, painters, filmmakers, and writers—these mountains, water, forests, and creatures have had a profound impact on all the arts. The Maverick Festival is as integral to this place where I live as are the bluestone ridges, the bald eagles, and the Ashokan Reservoir.

Each Sunday I sit in the Maverick's rustic open-air sanctuary in the woods, transported by a wide array of world-class string quartets. Birdsong, cricket choirs, forest breezes, pattering rain, and crackling thunderstorms blend with violins and cellos, reflecting an intimate relationship between the land and the music. The program describes the colorful genesis of the festival: "'The Maverick' was the collective description for the colony of unabashed artists that flourished at the edge of Woodstock's artistic main drag from 1905 until about 1944: the term was both pejorative and affectionate. The Maverick Festival was an annual bacchanal conceived by Hervey White—founder and artistic elemental of the Maverick—as a Bohemian carnival to be held on the Colony's grounds under the August full moon."

The inimitable maverick spirit reflects that of the founder himself. A bearded social worker, poet, novelist, and utopian dreamer, Hervey White had survived crushing poverty on a Kansas farm to graduate from Harvard and become a socialist and early feminist. His passionate social consciousness informed the philosophy of the Maverick Arts Colony as well as what would eventually become the music festival. In contrast to the cultured, aristocratic Ralph Radcliffe Whitehead, who founded the nearby Byrdcliffe Arts Colony, Hervey White was backwoods bohemian, sporting tight bicycle pants and a red necktie in honor of his socialist leanings. For two years Hervey worked for Ralph Whitehead, helping to oversee the construction of the roads and buildings of Byrdcliffe. But eventually the strong differences in both their personalities and their visions—wealthy privilege versus populist inclusivity—drove them apart and led Hervey White to build his own community. It was the sheer force of Hervey's ethical idealism, artistic vision, and charisma that brought the best musicians from New York, Boston, Philadelphia, and Minneapolis to the tiny rustic village of Woodstock to perform in the woods without pay. Here they became part of the Maverick's emerging art colony with its experimental communal living and exploding creativity.

Before long White purchased a printing press, which allowed him to print concert programs as well as to start *The Maverick Press*, which published poems, plays, novels, and Hervey's progressive literary monthly that went on to become *The Plowshare*. The very first program states that the concerts would be dedicated to, "The highest class of all music, known as chamber music. Performed every Sunday at 4:00 in the afternoon, with tea served afterwards. Admission: 25 cents."

The name 'Maverick' is also part of the Hervey White legend. Story has it that as a youth in 1890 Hervey visited his sister's Colorado farming commune, where he heard tales about a white stallion that roamed wild in the canyons. The image haunted his psyche and White resolved to call his colony Maverick to symbolize "a passion for free, unfettered living." Today John Flannagan's iconic eighteen-foot-tall chestnut sculpture of the maverick horse is the centerpiece of the concert hall.

Now one-hundred-years-old, the Maverick Festival and the spirit of its founder are alive and well. The festival continues to draw the highest caliber string quartets, and for the past twenty-five years I have been a devotee. How I love the intimacy of this music with its innate equality between the individual members of the quartet rendering this a quintessentially democratic form. And the musicians are still enamored with the rustic setting which remains pretty much the way Hervey White built it, a pastoral music chapel in the woods boasting acoustics that can compete with Carnegie Hall's. A perfect venue for chamber music, the intimate hall continues to accommodate fewer than two hundred, and Hervey's outside free seating endures. Audiences still stamp their feet on the floor to show ardent appreciation for the musicians, begging them to return for encores.

This afternoon this valley was surely as elated as I was by the Borromeo String Quartet playing Bach, Beethoven, and Dvorak. With the perfect balance of technique and passion, the quartet's musicianship seemed to reflect both the constancy and fluidity of these bluestone mountains. So moving was their rendition of Dvorak's String Quartet No. 13 that I can still feel the music affecting my body, my emotions, and my spirit. I see so clearly why both music and landscape are essential sanctuaries for me. I sense, too, the ineffable and intimate exchange between them. Certainly this valley—mountains, sky, forests, and creatures—has inspired and restored the members of the Borromeo. And surely this string quartet's music has fully inundated the hills and dales, the reservoir and eagle's peninsula, and the bluestone ridges and treetops of this place.

Now walking here along the Ashokan Way, the Borromeo's sublime interpretation of the Bach fugue comes pouring back over me and I feel the Maverick spirit filling every cell of my body. Hervey White's mandate—to live free and unfettered; to dream and take wild chances, to deepen in social consciousness, to lead with ethical idealism, and to be uplifted by the pure pleasure of creativity—lives deep inside this mountain valley, and it resides deep inside me, too.

Owls on the Full Moon

It's a full moon, the corn moon, on this hot dry evening. Driving home alone after dinner with a friend, I can't resist stopping at the reservoir. And there, rising above the Ashokan, is a perfect apricot moon. A full chorus of crickets and peepers greets me along with the fireflies and moonlight. Fishing boats with their night lanterns sparkle in the water. In the moon's silver light, I see a lone burst of red maple, like flames amidst the forest. The mountains have assumed their nighttime personality, their inky silhouettes against the blue-black sky somehow conferring them with even more gravitas than they possess during daytime hours. And then my favorite night sound on these Ashokan shores— the hoot of an owl—connects me with the non-physical world and my longing to understand where I came from. Plentiful here, owls have always been my messengers from the unseen, urging me to understand my role in the cosmos.

The owl is hooting, the full moon is shimmering, and I am imbibing the deep quiet of this mountain basin. I can feel that at the very beginning there was only this silence, absolutely nothing but this radiant silence. And then came the primal moment when matter joined the quiet. Over millennia this very landscape was born, eons and eons before humans were here. For all that time this land has lived in stillness, and over these last decades it has witnessed me with its calm presence. And it will be here, quietly, long after I am gone. I share these silent origins with the mountains, water, sky, and creatures. And our mutual belonging to this stillness is an essential part of my kinship with the landscape.

Of all the ample gifts of landscape, perhaps the most precious is silence. In fact, I cannot fathom who I would be without the nourishment of this quiet. So precious is this gift that it feels to me like an element in and of itself. I sense that I cannot truly hear anything—music, birdcalls, laughter, or what another person is really saying to me—unless I can also experience silence. Sound and silence form two halves of a whole, their complementarity so profound that one cannot exist without the other. They stand as icons of being and nonbeing, fullness and emptiness. The landscape is constantly demonstrating this fundamental balance—the quiet space surrounding birdsong, the earth's silent presence housing the gurgling sounds of rivers and streams, the still sand receiving the sea's lapping waves.

I reflect on what happens to me when I don't have enough silence. I become so full that there is no longer space for the existence of the person I aspire to be—the me who has proper perspective on life; the one who can respond in caring, generous ways to those I love and work with; the person who seeks meaning even in the most difficult circumstances; the me who is connected to beauty and a sense of the sacred. When crowded out by too much sound, stimulation, information, doing, and talking, this aspiring me is buried alive. But at any time the landscape can rescue my essential nature by gently reminding me of the eons of silence from which it came, and from which I, too, originated.

Sitting here alone tonight, I give myself fully to this vast ancient stillness. I feel this land patiently offering me its silence, my original place of belonging. There is nothing more comforting, nothing more sustaining.

A Love Affair's Lineage

After the heat wave breaks, everyone is out enjoying this clear dry summer day. Runners, walkers, roller bladers, and bikers of every variety—including parents pulling small covered contraptions containing their beaming children—fill the Ashokan Way. It's a symphony of movement and happiness. Nearing the eagle's peninsula, I see that people have paused to watch a mother with her two fawns drinking at the reservoir's edge. The water's perfect reflection of the deer family is a showstopper. And when the eagle lifts off from his nest soaring way out on the reservoir and up over these bluestone peaks, I can feel that all of us watching are lifted, too. I continue on my way, reveling in the daisies and clover, Irish lace and yarrow. The chicory has never seemed so abundant and I want to wrap myself in its rich periwinkle color. Seeing a cloud of burgundy dragonflies with their transparent wings flittering among the chicory, I recognize this variety as band-winged meadowhawk. Then and there, I decide that I, too, would like to be a meadowhawk dragonfly on this particular summer morning.

Surrounded by so many people under the spell of the Ashokan Way, I am thinking about the first line of *A Sand County Almanac*, Aldo Leopold's seminal work on place: "There are some who can live without wild things, and some who cannot." All of us here today are being restored and uplifted by the mountains, water, forests, and creatures of this protected space. But what will happen if people no longer have contact with the wild? I contemplate when it was that I first knew I couldn't live without the natural world, and how that recognition led me to living in this valley and walking daily along Ashokan Way. Could it be that there is an inexorable line connecting my earliest love affair with nature to this very place where I have spent my entire adulthood?

Among my most distinct childhood memories are endless hours spent outdoors near our home in Wilmington, Delaware in the Brandywine River Valley. An intrepid tomboy, I loved everything about being out in nature. Younger by only fourteen months, my sister Joanie was my constant comrade in exploring the territory where we lived. We were often mistaken as twins and indeed we were inseparable. Dressed in scruffy blue jeans and red striped tee shirts with our identical Dutch boy haircuts, we were two rascals looking for trouble.

Shinnying our skinny legs way up over trunks and out onto long branches, we veritably explored every tree in our childhood landscape. We especially loved the sprawling old beech tree at the end of our yard whose boughs reached out over the small brook called the Pancake Run. After hanging upside down like monkeys in the old tree, we followed the Pancake Run down to the Brandywine River with its old stone mills. Along the Pancake Run we collected stores of treasure: pebbles, moss, bark, and insects. In the winter we took big sticks and broke the ice; as spring arrived we made bouquets of the wild violets lining the shores of the brook. We cooled off our feet in the run in summer, and in autumn we collected bright red and yellow leaves that we would later press under wax paper. No matter what the season, we arrived at the Brandywine drenched and filthy, feeling no less important than Lewis and Clark. That trip down the Pancake Run to the Brandywine River was the Ashokan Way of my childhood.

As so many siblings do, Joanie and I had our share of vicious fights but our conflicts rarely took place when we were out in the landscape. And like all families, ours had its darkness: the tension of my mother's mysterious illness that led to her early death at the age of fifty-five; the constant financial strain of a family

of five living on my father's teacher's salary; and the inevitable
marital stress between my parents that came from always strug-
gling to make ends meet. But the natural world was my refuge.
And though I have no words for my experience out in nature,
as a child I knew that I felt alive when I was outside, part of a
throbbing interconnected web of life. I knew that if I was sad,
or mad, or confused when I started out that I would feel better when I returned home soaked with the water of my beloved
brook, my pockets full of talismans from the land that I knew like
the back of my own hand. By the time I was six-years-old, I knew
I couldn't live without regular excursions into the natural world.

Later when I was around ten, there came the summers at
Camp Ettowah deep in the Maine woods. Called the Skunk
Cabin, our rustic lodging sat on the shores of Kimball Pond with
the entire outline of Mount Kearsarge prominent in our view.
From eight in the morning until bedtime at nine, Joanie and
I explored the creeks and sandy shorelines, canoed and swam,
discovered loons and bullfrogs, walked the long dirt roads with
their canopy of birch, maple, and pine, and grinned with mouths
stained dark purple by wild blueberries. Venturing into the pine
forests, we collected scented needles for the fragrant balsam pil-
lows that mom had taught us how to make. And under our father's guidance we hiked difficult trails and grew strong, falling
in love with the White Mountains along the way. We lived all
day in the wild until our mother would finally drag us inside to
sleep. During those Maine summers, I was on the Ashokan Way
all day long.

When Joanie grew up, she became a wetlands ecologist and an
award-winning nature poet. And I created a home in the Hudson River Valley that so closely mimics the Maine landscape of
my childhood that the only explanation for this can be true love.
Somehow I knew that stored in my visceral memory of that land
was a blueprint for my happiness. Just slightly softening my gaze,

I can look out from my house and watch the Ashokan Reservoir become Kimball Pond while High Point shape shifts into Mount Kearsarge. I am both a girl of ten and a woman of sixty-eight who knows that she cannot live without the wild. And I pray that each of us can find our way to be in regular contact with some aspect of the natural world, that each of us can understand how much our humanity depends on this notion.

AUTUMN

SEPTEMBER

TRANSMUTE THE WOUND INTO LIGHT

After spending the day in New York City, I am now strolling into the Ashokan's soft evening dusk and reflecting on my experience. Just hours ago I walked the city's teeming streets. In the space of three blocks, I saw more people than I might encounter in an entire month living here in the country. People of every color, size, nationality, personality, and dress were crowded around me, and I easily discerned at least five or six languages. Shouting, rushing, pushing, arguing, and laughing, this sea of humanity poured down the avenues like a giant unstoppable river. I almost felt as if I no longer needed to move on my own accord because the city's momentum itself was propelling me forward. At each block I inhaled the thick aroma of ethnic foods mixed with gasoline exhaust and human sweat. The sheer motion and energy gave me the kind of adrenaline rush that I don't experience living in a rural setting. I arrived at Lincoln Center, one of my favorite places in New York, to find it more crowded than I had ever seen it, with cameras everywhere. It's Fashion Week and all around me gorgeous models turned to offer their radiant smiles to this astonishing city. I escaped into a quiet restaurant for brunch with friends before the theater.

Because I don't live in New York, its richness stands out in bas-relief against the quiet simplicity of my surroundings, shocking my senses with its vitality and audacity. And because I often go in and out of the city on the same day for business meetings or cultural events, I have thought a lot about living inside the contrasts between New York and the Ashokan Way. Now walking

here alone, it is the stillness and space that shock my senses. The
Ashokan's vast openness is as awe inspiring as the density of the
city's streets, and its calm affects me as deeply as the surging energy of surging energy of the crowds. I am well aware of what
past people of this mountain valley sacrificed to New York City.
I know that even today, some feel that the Ashokan is a reminder
as well as a requiem to all those who forever lost their land and
their way of life.

It was my neighbor the artist Kate McGloughlin who first
articulated what I had long been feeling but didn't have words
for—that the Ashokan's beauty is elegiac.

"The weird thing about the Ashokan Reservoir," she once
told me, "is that some of my people used to live in one of the
towns formerly located where the water rests today. They were
forced to leave their land and the beautiful farm and gristmill
they owned to make room for the reservoir, which was needed
to provide drinking water for the other half of my family, who
came to New York from Ireland with the thirsty multitude that
descended here in an enormous wave."

Kate's ancestors' paradoxical relationship to the Ashokan
places us deep inside the creative tension surrounding this landscape. A quarter of a mile from the main dam of the Ashokan
Reservoir underneath 180 feet of water lie the foundations of
Bishop Falls, the gristmill and stone house that Kate's ancestor
Asa Bishop built here in 1790. Somewhere else under the water, sit the remains of the home, bluestone quarry, and general
store belonging to the parents of Kate's great-grandmother Bessie Bishop.

"I knew my great-grandmother, Bessie Bishop Davis, and I
can tell you she never got over the loss," Kate says. "When my
brother and I were kids we used to ask her where she grew up
and she always replied, 'I grew up under the reservoir.' She was
98 when she died, and was still pissed that they 'stole her home'."

So, how can a place that holds this much grief be a place that provides an equal measure of peace and inspiration to so many people? There's more to it than the ever-changing aesthetic hit of mountain, water, and sky. I think the story, itself an elegy, lays a thick layer of beauty-born-of-tragedy on this place, and I'm sure that's the real thing that people respond to when they visit the Ashokan Reservoir."

Like me, Kate lives less than a mile from the Ashokan. Her Olivebridge home and studio, built by her grandfather Alonzo Davis, are just across from the stone farmhouse where Bessie Bishop lived with her husband, the dairy farmer Lester Davis, on the crossroads of Davis Corners. Much of Kate's art is a tribute to this place and to her people, some long gone and some still alive. The first time I saw her paintings of this mountain valley, I was struck speechless. There in front of me was the visual embodiment of what I had been writing about these past years. There before me the Ashokan Way unfolded in all its moods: clear and ebullient, mist filled and downhearted, elusive and shy, commanding and charismatic. There in Kate's infinite hues of blues, purples, and grays was my familiar High Point Mountain, just as it had appeared to me in my dreams. Spread across her canvases, the ever-changing water and sky were so evocative that I longed to step into the paintings, to be restored by their infinite space.

Sitting with Kate surrounded by her artwork of the place we both love, I once asked her what she feels when she's on the Ashokan Way? " I feel rapture but not joy. I have big feelings, and it's big beauty up on the reservoir. And when I paint this place I feel the melancholy. The amazing thing is that it is never, ever the same. The light is always changing, ever engaging. It's always new to me. The light is the whole thing."

This evening, wrapped in the Ashokan's soft dusk, I am absorbed in Kate's words about the light. Now I see that they offer me a way to understand the paradox of this place. Like the light, both life and landscape are always changing. This reservoir was completed almost a century ago and I have been walking here for almost forty years. By now I am part of a changing chapter of Ashokan history, one where people thrive on the radical contrast between the dense complexity of New York's urban landscape and the wide-open stillness of this protected mountain valley. The tension that tore apart another generation is for me a tension that enhances creativity, rendering me more alive and curious about the human condition. To be able to visit New York City and then return home to walk along this place of many fishes is an immeasurable blessing.

This landscape is remarkably magnanimous, holding the past next to the present while allowing a place for the future. My pleasure in this land and the sorrows of those who lost their homes mingle together, colored somehow by the unknown, and perhaps unimaginable, stories of those yet to come. All this renders this place more evocative, more representative of the complexity of our human condition. And part of the intrinsic power out here in the Ashokan's open space is that there is ample room for all of this.

As I walk into the twilight that converts these mountains into a deep blue, I hear Jung's mandate to transmute the wound into light. I am reminded that this purposeful transmutation—this purposeful changing of one thing into another—is an essential part of our humanness. I feel sure that Kate's luminous paintings, connected to her ancestral line, have honored the pain here as well as transforming it into light.

AUTUMN EQUINOX
THE DELICIOUS NEARBY FREEDOM OF DEATH

Today is the autumn equinox, and fall wraps itself around me with a blustery wind. In the field below, grasses turn burgundy and amber. Asters dot the hillsides like violet stars. Along the lower ridges and hollows, the hardwood forests display wide sweeps and curves of yellow, as if a giant calligraphy brush had painted its strokes across the mountain range. A lone maple tree flaunts a spiral of brilliant colors: a lower ring of emerald green leaves followed by loops of yellow and orange, then a ring of fiery red spiraling to the top, bursting into the sky like flames escaping to heaven.

Here on this opening day of autumn I am experiencing the natural polar opposite of the spring equinox. Instead of spring red buds inching across this valley heralding so much green birth, September's colorful leaves usher in winter's nakedness followed by death. Out here on the Ashokan Way, birth and death exist in an open, natural manner as two halves of a whole circle, rounding each other out with no false separation, no clinging to life and pushing away death. I am thinking a lot about these themes as soon I will launch a new year-long training on conscious aging. And these reflections permeate my psyche as I enter the late September of my life.

In my aging, I aspire to fully enter into the paradoxical terrain of decay and wisdom, revolt and adaptation, denial and acceptance. I want to greet the changes of growing old as opportunities for spiritual maturation and meaning. In our youth-obsessed culture, there is scant encouragement for this. But the landscape does foster this inquiry in rich and informative ways. When I pay attention to the natural world, it eloquently embodies the teaching that life on this dualistic plane is nothing but complementary opposites: light and dark, visible and invisible, full and empty, sound and silence, male and female, life and death. And with its incomparable ability to inhabit the present moment, nature apparently says to me: Death will come to you in its own time, so why not really live now? Why not leap empty-handed into the depths of this messy, fertile, paradox of getting old?

In our society, one of the most subversive problems in aging is a dementia of the imagination. So many cultural assumptions conspire to shrink our creativity, short-circuiting unforeseen epiphanies and unfettered wisdom. Dried up, closed in, and hidden away in nursing homes, older people lose access to their interior open space; this is one of the reasons that contact with the natural world is so essential in our later years. Nature's divine imagination inspires curiosity and a beginner's mind, expansive thinking and a sense of wonder—all of which foster creativity. The wild and unexpected aspects of landscape encourage us, even in unconscious or unarticulated ways, to open to the wild and unexpected places in ourselves. Where do my untamed and unpredictable instincts lead me? With a vital imagination I could easily view death the way Walt Whitman did in *Song of the Open Road.* "Old age flowing free with the delicious nearby freedom of death." Out on the open road I could reinvent myself in surprising ways that help sustain meaning and joy in the autumn of my life.

Since aging is one of the great teachers of change, then part of my spiritual practice in these later years is to engage with what does not change. My body is changing, my mind is forgetting more, my work is shifting, I am losing those I love, and death is nearer for me. But what is constant? The landscape's steady, humble presence is an enormous comfort. Just sitting in this mountain valley, breathing in the primal silence, gives me a profound experience of constancy. With its capacity to simultaneously hold the past, present, and future, this land transcends linear time and space. It offers the vision of an ineffable realm beyond time. When I am gone this faithful place will still hold the memory of me with the invisible echoes of my footsteps. As I grow older, this landscape's primordial continuity bestows the kindest of benedictions.

I have made it known that when I die I want my ashes scattered here, along the Ashokan Way. But until that time comes, I would like to enter this September of my life as if I am like the bright autumn colors that come before the nakedness of death. I wish to engage with the vibrant youth around me as if they are the fresh new green of spring, and I am the rich palette of autumn offering my cycles of experience. In these coming years as I lose more and more of my color, I want to experience this as the natural preparation for my death. And when I take my last breath, I hope to imagine myself as a bare winter tree lying on the forest floor, my naked grey skeleton becoming one with the earth that nurtured my life.

WOODSTOCK'S LANDSCAPE
AND ITS EFFECT ON THE SOUL

What is it about this place that magnetizes painters, writers, musicians, filmmakers, philosophers, and mavericks of every stripe? What exactly is the magic of this valley? These are the questions I am pondering as I walk the shores of the Ashokan on this soft, warm autumn evening.

I've spent the afternoon at the Woodstock School of Art's (WSA) comprehensive show entitled *The Woodstock Landscape Then and Now*, curated by my neighbor and WSA President Kate Mc-Gloughlin. Spanning more than a century of works, the paintings were stirringly familiar to me with their renderings of the fields, forests, streams, sky, and mountains that I have loved over these past three decades. How marvelous to see my familiar outer landscape come inside on canvases, and come inside me in new ways. Bolton Brown's luminous pink, lavender, blue, and green images transform immediately recognized Catskill ridges and hollows into living, breathing forms. If I could paint, what color would I use to depict these beloved shapes? In Robert Angeloch's *Wet October*, his autumn woods are so visceral that I can feel the rain sparkling on the oak trees and smell the musty odor of the forest floor. Am I inside a beautiful gallery, or am I outside in the woods on a rainy day? And so familiar is the landscape of Mary Anna Goetz's *Sickler Road* that I know each tree and each section of the field on the canvas, and my feet have hiked every inch of the purple mountain slopes she has brought inside these walls. I stand for a long time in front of her painting, allowing the beauty to wash over me, and allowing myself to remember the very first time that I hiked this landscape, feeling as if I had already known it for a long time.

And now, walking the Ashokan Way directly into the landscape so often portrayed by Woodstock artists, I am thinking about how I have fallen under the spell of this valley. There are so many beautiful locations in the world and I have visited more than my share of them. But this place seems to imprint the psyche in such a way that it invites a person to write about it, paint or film it, or compose music. Like so many others before me, I, too, long to capture the effect of this landscape on my soul.

That the magnetism of this place is still so strong long after John Burroughs wrote about it and Thomas Cole, Frederick Church, and others memorialized it through the Hudson River Valley School of Painting is compelling to me. Today we have Woodstock music, art, film, and writer's festivals at every turn of the season.

Falling in love with this mountain valley, creative people of all stripes quickly discover that the landscape thoroughly invades the psyche, inhabiting dreamscapes with vivid archetypal symbols. During a period of unchecked workaholism when I was no longer writing, I dreamt that I left my bed to fly directly over to High Point. I enter a cave in the mountainside where there was a small writing desk with pen and paper. A turning point, the dream through the portal of my beloved mountain helped return me to my creative source. So often the landscape, both literally as well as symbolically, guides us to retrieve our deepest yearnings. It reminds us what offers lasting meaning and how easy it is to abandon this when we are swallowed by life's stresses and distractions.

Whether the land enhances an already existing creative endeavor or returns us to the source of our inspiration, the writers, painters, musicians, and filmmakers of this mountain valley want to be out in the very midst of this landscape. And then after walking in these ancient bluestone mountains, sitting near the rushing streams, or lying in the open fields with the sky as a ceiling, comes the desire to offer something back for all that the land has so freely given. There is a natural longing to give concrete form—words, colors, images, or musical notes—to the beauty that sustains our soul. Our connection to the land is so many different things—muse, strength, prayer, and humanity. And I have come to believe that it is the ongoing exchange between the landscape and the artists who honor it through their chosen form that sustains not just individual artists' souls, but the very soul of this valley. For all these artists, their reverence for this landscape is part of the long body of this place, joining them with those who went before and those who will come after.

OCTOBER

Nature, Art, and Spirituality Meet Their Strange Bedfellow: Technology

It's a bright morning and each day now the valley's hardwood forests display more of their autumn palette of amber, pumpkin, ochre, and burgundy. The yellow hues are so vibrant up on High Point that the entire mountain appears to be glowing. On the way south for the winter, large flocks of geese have begun their pass over the Ashokan. Jubilant honking is followed by a loud swoosh as dozens of birds land on the surface of the water, a sequence of sounds so sublime to my ears that a deep contentment settles over me. It is a perfect day for walking, and a wonderful line by the poet Antonio Machado comes to mind: "*No hay camino, se hace camino al andar.*" *There is no road, the road is made by walking.*

Today I am contemplating the trinity of nature, art, and spirituality. For many, there is an intrinsic link between our connection to the natural world, our creativity, and our sense of the sacred. These three forces form a living circle where each one nurtures the other. If we abandon our intimate relationship with the landscape, we risk losing some of our imagination as well as our sense of the divine. Part of the reason why the creative arts and myriad spiritual centers thrive in this ancient mountain valley is that many of the people who live here are deeply connected to the land. When a painter, filmmaker, or writer engages with the land they find themselves spiritually uplifted as well as creatively restored. The lines between art, landscape, and spiritual practice disappear. It's also true that the circle turns both ways; as artists pay homage to the land and as seekers engage with nature as part of their contemplative practice, then the landscape itself is reflected and enriched.

This year's first offering at the "fiercely independent" Woodstock Film Festival was *To Be Forever Wild*. Created by local filmmakers, musicians, and artists, this work in progress celebrates the Catskills and its people. A montage of mountains, streams, waterfalls, and open skies along with artists of every stripe, and seekers from various traditions including a lively Tibetan monk who has settled in this valley, the film was a prayer, as well as a plea, that we all act to assure that this area remain wild and protected. The young director David Becker teaches at the Woodstock Day School and I could feel his love for this place in every frame of his film.

The film struck a deep chord in me. At first I was filled with happiness that I am lucky enough to live in this valley, but then a dreadful worry came over me. How will our world's increasing loss of connection to the natural world affect both our psyches and our open spaces? I am one of a rising number of people who believe that our epidemic addiction to electronic devices threatens to sever some essential part of our humanity. In countless ways we're always connected, but too many of us feel separate at the deepest existential level, where real meaning lives. We're all obese with information overload, but we're still hungry ghosts. Technology is here to stay and I am glad for that. But how do we balance our technology with our humanness? The trinity of nature, art, and spirituality offers a circuit breaker, a way to disrupt our technology trance.

All three of these are pathways into true belonging, connecting us to something larger than ourselves, something more sustaining. When hiking a mountain, painting a watercolor, or sitting in meditation, linear time seems to disappear. The self-centered ego drops away and we become the right size—not too big, but not too small. Space opens up inside us and we feel both calmer and stronger. Each of these practices returns us to a slower rhythm, nourishing our interior lives. Now we are fed by, and connected to, sources deep within ourselves, yet simultaneously linked to an immense universe. When the inevitable, difficult life initiations come our way—illness, divorce, loss, betrayal, depression, or death—these three pathways can help sustain us.

It's no mistake that contact with the natural world, participation in any art form, and engagement with any kind of spiritual practice mutually reinforce each other. Each one of these alone can help us break our addiction to technology, each one can inspire us to protect our open spaces. But the unified force field of landscape, the arts, and spiritual practice can help ensure that our earth, along with all of us living here, stay forever wild.

BEING IN LOVE
AS INSIDE AND OUTSIDE DISAPPEAR

Never do I remember such a string of halcyon days as these last two weeks have given us. I simply do not have enough words for this mountain valley's October colors, but I can smell and taste their spicy mix: ginger, cinnamon, cayenne, turmeric, and mustard. The cerulean sky seems to go on forever, reminding me that the native Esopus people called this valley *Onteora*, land of the sky. And down below, the grassy fields have changed into their autumn coat of amber and lavender, while out on the tip of the eagle's peninsula a stand of maples is such a vibrant crimson that I wait for the forest to suddenly be engulfed in flames.

All week long I have abandoned my desk, unabashedly playing hooky, imbibing the splendor of this landscape. Longing to merge with it, to become it. And often enough, I am blessed to find this communion. Watching the great blue heron soaring across the Ashokan, I am acutely aware of its unique honking sound as I track its path until I can no longer see it. The heron's flight has taken over my consciousness; nothing else exists. The outer landscape has come inside me.

Even after the heron has vanished, the memory of the winged one stays inside me for a long time: the utter grace and magnitude of its wingspan, its primordial sound and shape, my ancient longing to know what it would feel like to fly with the bird, and the mystery of where it is going and when I will see it again—all these things work on me in profound ways that don't concern my rational brain, but that are essential for my primal consciousness.

This is consciousness where there is no separation between the heron and me.

On the innumerable occasions when my mountain familiar High Point has shown me its own interior—sadness stored in hollows on a dark day, secrets revealed as mists lift off ledges, rigid contours transformed into softness after a snowstorm, and indomitable fidelity throughout the seasons—I, too, am encouraged to find these very places inside myself. My interior disappears inside High Point's interior. For more than three decades, this continual exchange between High Point and me has shaped us as intimates, and I know for the years that I have left this mountain will continue to rearrange me and put back together. Between myself and the mountain, I no longer know which is inside and which outside.

For ancients, the West's sense of separation between human and nature didn't exist, nor does it exist for most indigenous peoples today. Their sensibility lives outside the realm of words and concepts in the realm of poets, mystics, and shamans. To merge with an aspect of the landscape, I have to shift out of the rigid boundaries of my human ego and enter a more permeable place. This shift is very similar to what takes place during spiritual practice when the mind calms, allowing one's singular identity to blend with a larger field of awareness. Though I will never have the acute sensitivity of an indigenous person who has spent his or her entire life in intimate relationship with the land, my admiration for this landscape is enough to allow our inside and outside to become indistinguishable.

On this glorious October day along the Ashokan Way I am glad that I no longer feel the boundaries between myself and this mountain valley. I am suddenly certain that this is what love is. Anyone who has experienced this kind of union with an aspect of the landscape knows that they are left refreshed, enlarged, and more fully human. And as I have so often wondered about this mutual exchange between human and nature, is the land then rendered more itself, more completely mountain like? But being in a state of love quickly dispenses with such rational considerations and I simply allow the bright azure sky to swallow me up and the spicy mixture of autumn's colors to intoxicate me as I disappear inside this place.

KNIGHTOWER

CIRCLING AROUND AN IMPOSSIBLE DREAM

Today I am taking my walk by way of the Knightower, a forty-three-foot tall structure less than two miles from my house. My neighbor Barry Knight built it, and his story has become a legend in this valley. A photographer by trade, Barry heard about an abandoned fire tower in the town of Esperance. Originally built in the 1940s, the tower had been moved several times and was in use until the end of the fire tower era in the 1970s. When Barry first saw the tower in 2002, it lay scattered in hundreds of pieces in the mud and grass. But at that moment his impossible dream to rebuild the tower—which ultimately amounted to building his own tower—was born. And rebuild it he did; steel bar by steel bar, bolt by bolt, level by level, and step-by-step. Because the metal had oxidized over the years, Barry had to hand clean, prime, and coat each original piece with aluminum paint. Never has the term "a labor of love" been more apt than for the construction of the Knightower.

In his matter-of-fact way, Barry describes what was required for his labor of love.

"When I first saw what would become my tower, I had to scour the entire landscape, digging and pulling pieces out of the mud and clinging grasses. I couldn't afford to miss a single piece. There was a huge mound of nuts, bolts, and washers all mixed in the mud. I used eight enormous buckets to transport this metal and mud soup back to my house. Everything in the eight buckets had to be rinsed five times in clear water because of the mud. Then the sorting began. There were seven different sizes of bolts, each used on a different part of the tower. During football season, I sat on my couch watching the games and scraping the dirt out of the threads of each nut and bolt with a wire brush. Was I crazy? Some people thought so. But I must admit that at no point during this entire project did I ever feel, think, or say in a negative mindset, ' Why am I doing this? ' Onward! Always forward!"

"I grew up on this land and up in back of my house is all wooded forest which crests along a three-mile ridge that is now named Ashokan Ridge," Barry says.

"Miles of trails take you all over this land and down into a valley that extends all the way to the reservoir. As children, my sisters and I loved to play here, chasing each other and climbing trees. We called this place Mountain Top and this is where I chose to build my dream tower."

Just before we leave his house to climb Knightower, Barry describes the moment he first witnessed the panorama from atop the tower back before it was completed, and before there was a steady iron ladder with guardrails like there is now. "With all the fabricated steel supports installed, I hauled two platform boards up and onto the deck level. I crawled off the extension ladder onto these two planks and there was nothing around me except a forty-foot drop. From my knees I stood up slowly and panned the view for the first time. It was beyond my expectations. The Ashokan Reservoir spread out along the base of the Southern Catskills, onto the Shawangunk Mountains and the Mohonk Mountain House. I could see the Olana Estate near the town of Hudson some twenty-five miles away. It was spectacular and I wanted others to be able to enjoy it. It was time to get back to work."

When we arrive at the base of the lofty structure, my neighbor rings a large bell to welcome me, an ancient signal that I am passing over a threshold into a sacred place. Then we begin our climb, spiraling up and up, forty feet into the sky. Atop the tower, my vertigo is both physical and spiritual. Just as Barry had described to me, I can see the entire Catskill Mountain watershed, and the site's immensity does wild things to my imagination. Up here in the sky's etheric domain, earthly concepts such as time disappear.

Looking out on the vast expanse of the valley where I walk every day, I fall under the spell of its three-hundred-million-year evolution. Over eons and eons, waters advanced and receded, lands rose and fell, and as the earth became swampy, huge plants and dinosaurs inhabited this place. When the ice came like a colossal white giant, it carved out the mountain ranges spread before me like massive waves in a cosmic ocean. And the waves of this valley's history continued to unfold: the native Esopus people fished and hunted, the Dutch farmers cut their roads, giant mule wagons carried hides up from the Hudson River on to tanneries, huge slabs of bluestone were dragged down the mountainsides by oxen, the railroad came, the last handmade dam was constructed, and thousands of people fled their farms as their villages were blasted and burned away. And now, the Ashokan Reservoir rises up before me. The echoes and shadows, voices and stories of all that has gone before form the long body of this place, and I am now a part of that long body, too.

Way up here atop Barry's impossible dream, the veil is decidedly thin and it seems completely natural that landscape holds multiple eras of history in plain sight. Barry is a great storyteller, and his words bring me back into the present moment. A history buff, he tells me that he has recited the Gettysburg address so often up here that he's sure the deer, fox, bear, owl, eagle, and whip-poor-will who inhabit the *Ashokan Ridge* might know the words by now. He calls out the names of twenty-four prominent Catskill peaks spread before us and tells me that there are thirty- six species of trees in this ledge's forest. If you are standing in this tower that lives in the sky, at certain times of year, massive flocks of migrating birds fly so near that you can almost touch them. Rehabilitated owls and hawks have been released back into the wild from here. On clear nights the stars appear so close and so abundant that Barry sleeps up here informed by the vastness that surrounds him. And he describes a special time when a musician friend climbed the tower, took up his fiddle and played a haunting rendition of the famous song *Ashokan Farewell.*

Finally we both are quiet, and I can clearly hear Rilke's poem about the ancient tower.

> *I live my life in growing orbits*
> *that move out over the world.*
> *perhaps I can never achieve the last,*
> *but that will be my attempt.*
> *I am circling around God, around the ancient tower,*
> *and I have been circling for a thousand years,*
> *and I still don't know if I am a falcon, or a storm,*
> *or a great song.*

Soon it's time to go. We climb down, down, down the tower's ladder where at the bottom Barry once again rings the big bell. The vibrating sound helps me to shift from the sky's ethereal domain back down to solid ground. But prompted by Rilke's poem, I find myself circling and circling around Knightower for the rest of the day, around Barry's labor of love, around an impossible dream come true, and around this *Ashokan Ridge* that I call home.

November

Just Like You,
I Want to be Happy.
Just Like You,
I Want to be Free of Suffering.

With the vivid foliage gone, this valley is all muted hues of pumpkin and peach. The mountains are the color of adobe, reminding me of the skyline in Santa Fe. The dying fern forests, now burnt umber, dare me to have faith that they will be reborn. On their way south a flock of geese rests in an Ashokan cove. When they plunge headfirst into the reservoir, their ample white bottoms wag in the air, their down feathers ruffling and then scattering in the wind. In contrast to the showy communal geese, a solitary loon way out on the mudflats offers her haunting call.

The air is rich with the smell of wood smoke and dead leaves flutter to the ground like confetti in a parade. Their crunching underfoot is a sound that has always announced the final phase of autumn for me. We are all preparing for winter now, for the time of dying.

Indeed, this is All Soul's Day, a day to pray for the dead. Across the globe, bells ring, candles burn, and soul cakes are baked for those who have passed from this earth. In Mexico, many people believe that the spirits of the dead return to enjoy a visit with their family and relatives on this day, *Día de los Muertos*. But today I am not so much thinking of those who I have lost—my parents and my brother, dear friends, students, and colleagues. Rather I find myself pondering all that the world has lost, and is losing.

An inevitable consequence of contemplating loss, I am also reflecting on suffering. I know about the thousands of extinguished species, the vanishing rainforests, and the disappearing polar ice cap. Every day the news reports on the alarming spread of terrorism, of people planting bombs or shooting into crowds or blowing themselves up in order to kill those who are different than them. I have my own veritable library on genocide that includes books describing atrocities in Cambodia, Rwanda, Afghanistan, and Serbia. Next to these books sits my colleague Eve Ensler's seminal writing on female genital mutilation and the global epidemic of rape. And my own work is involved with sex trafficking, forced early marriage, all forms of violence against women, AIDS, and the desperate cycle of poverty. Is it because my Pop never talked about his unspeakable pain in watching his own father shoot himself that I have wanted to face and understand suffering and loss?

Just recently I read an interview with the author and activist Parker Palmer in which he said, "Violence is what happens when we don't know what else to do with our suffering." This sentence haunts me; it follows me everywhere. I am trying to comprehend what occurs when we don't feel and understand our own pain. It seems clear that when I reduce everything to a simple formula of us versus them, my way is right and your way is wrong, then it's easy to close my heart. I don't have to experience my own pain or anyone else's. And I don't have to face how complicated it is to be a human with all my own kindness and cruelty, which is, of course, a reflection of the world's light and shadow. Mature compassion, the opposite of violence, asks me not only to open my heart, but also my mind, which means then that I have to consider other people's ideas and beliefs. Perhaps an even subtler requirement of true empathy is open intention, or the practice of actually going toward what is different in order to try to understand it.

All this openness of heart, mind, and intention isn't easy. Mature compassion isn't for the fainthearted. It requires us to be large enough to hold many opposites, multiple creative tensions of values, beliefs, and points of view, some that we agree with and some that we don't. Asked what prayer he turned to when he was tempted to judge another, the Dalai Lama said he repeated this simple line. "Just like you, I want to be happy. Just like you I want to be free of suffering." I find this profoundly helpful especially when I vehemently disagree with a person or a collective belief system. I can still say these words and mean them.

My attention returns to my landscape, the presence that has taught me most viscerally and most effectively about holding opposites. These mountains and forests, this sky and this water, are in a constant state of creative tension; sun and moon, dark and light, solid and fluid, life and death. I wonder what would happen if those prone to violence or imprisoned in fundamentalist worldviews were to spend ample time out in the natural world. Is it possible that an abundance of open space could open their hearts? Is it possible that the reconciliation of opposites inherent in landscape could help them to consider multiple points of view instead of just their own? Perhaps the land, which simultaneously holds the past and the present in equal regard, could teach them to honor both the lineage of what has come before and what is current now.

On this All Souls Day the landscape is preparing for winter, for the time of dying. No matter what beliefs we hold, all of us will have to go through the winters of our lives. And all of us will die. Returning home to my small meditation room, I ring a bell and light a candle, offering the prayer that all of us invite these words to live in our hearts: Just like you, I want to be happy. Just like you, I want to be free of suffering.

Thanksgiving Day
This Watcher's Journal Comes to An End

Though the lower ridges still hold some of their adobe glow, higher up in the dales and hollows these mountains are all boney grey. With the leaves gone, space has opened and the sky seems bigger. A slender crescent moon floats in the new spaciousness above, a small lone boat out to sea. Today's firmament is spectacular—long swathes of cornflower blue with massive puffy clouds crouching down along the horizon and settling into the lower valley. The reservoir is calm, and out on the mudflats, loons along with long-tailed yellow birds are hunkered down. Fragrant wood smoke wafts through the forests, leading me to imagine people content around their woodstoves and fireplaces. All this beauty gathers itself inside me and moves through me in waves of gratitude.

It is Thanksgiving Day, and this watcher's journal comes to an end one year after it began. It takes time to form intimate bonds with a place, for landscape to become a confidant, or what naturalists call a local patch. I have loved my local patch here along the Ashokan Way for thirty-six years. I have loved it not as a scientist or environmentalist, but as an ordinary person searching to make sense of modern life and to literally find my place in the world. Without a sense of place, it would be a daunting task to locate myself on this earth.

By now, with its own mythic force, this place has helped define who I am and what I believe. This sky and water, these mountains, forests, and creatures have entered every fiber of my imagination and my memory. Their tender loveliness along with their abiding presence has offered solace, perspective, and meaning to my life. This valley's three-hundred-million-year long body has reminded me how short my time here is, and that if I wish to leave an imprint, the time to do that is now. Walking the Ashokan Way has led me on a path of knowing beyond my intellect. A means of perception where mind, body, heart, and spirit join as one, similar to the way air, earth, water, and fire work together. With all aspects of my being in communion, I can enter the realms of the invisible and the timeless. The natural world awakens and unifies, it both grounds me and ushers me into the mystical. I am left both tranquil and trembling.

In *Walden*, Thoreau wrote, "I went to the woods because I wished to live deliberately, to front only the essential facts of life, and see if I could not learn what it had to teach, and not, when I came to die, discover that I had not lived." Here, in this single sentence, Thoreau has suggested to us not only why we might choose to live simply, but also how we might do it. Thoreau understood that landscape is essential to our humanity, that in caring for and protecting our open spaces we are in fact preserving our humanness. Without nature to witness and reflect us, to awaken and astonish us, to provide the water and air we need to survive, we are nothing.

I have done my best to pay attention and write down the elements that have touched me on my walks here along the Ashokan Way, though I know full well that words can never do justice to what I have witnessed or how this landscape has shaped me. Our local sage of Slabsides, John Burroughs, wrote, "Every place is under the stars, every place is the center of the world." But I think it is only when we have truly loved a place that it is then lit by the stars and it has then literally become the epicenter of one's world, informing imagination, memory, and sense of meaning. When I am gone I hope that others will love and care for this place. And perhaps we will meet here along the Ashokan Way, in that ineffable junction where the landscape holds the past, present, and future.

Acknowledgments

Editor extraordinaire Nan Satter, I am a better writer primarily because of you. We have worked together on several books and I am immeasurably blessed to have had you by my side. Ned Leavitt, thank you for your wise counsel through the years and for making this a better book. Leslie Browning, you are a dream to work with and Homebound Publications is the finest of homes for this book. I am so very grateful for your visionary approach to publishing. My neighbor Kate McGloughlin, your vision and your art allowed me to see what I had written. Your gifts have enriched both me, and, this book. Stephen Cope, dear friend thank you for honoring this book with your gracious foreword.

To these friends and family who read or listened to early versions of the manuscript and gave me the courage I needed: Joanie Mclean, Karen Watson, Ellen Wingard, Gunilla Norris, and Danit Fried.

To my sister Joanie McLean, thank you for the use of your exquisite poem "Remember This" which appeared in *New Millennium Writings*, Issue 24, 2015.

These books were invaluable to me in writing *The Ashokan Way*: Alf Evers' *Woodstock: History of an America Town*; Bob Steuding's *The Last of the Handmade Dams: The Story of the Ashokan Reservoir*; John Burrough's *In The Catskills*; Robert Macfarlane's *The Old Ways: A Journey on Foot*; Terry Tempest Williams' *An Unspoken Hunger*; Aldo Leopold's *A Sand County Almanac*; John O'Donohue's *Four Elements: Reflections on Nature*; and countless volumes of Mary Oliver's poetry.

And finally my gratitude to David: For all our walks along The Ashokan Way, and, for walking every step of the way with me.

ABOUT THE AUTHOR

GAIL STRAUB is the Executive Director of the Empowerment Institute, which she cofounded in 1981. As one of the world's leading authorities on women's empowerment, she codirects the Empowerment Institute's School for Transformative Social Change empowering change agents from around the world to design and implement cutting-edge social innovations. As part of this focus, she cofounded IMAGINE: A Global Initiative for the Empowerment of Women to help women heal from violence, build strong lives, and contribute to their community. IMAGINE initiatives are currently under way throughout Africa, Afghanistan, India, and the Middle East. Gail has consulted to many organizations furthering women's empowerment including the Chinese Women's Federation, Women for Women International, World Pulse, and the Omega Women's Leadership Center.

Gail is the author of five books including, with her husband David Gershon, the best-selling *Empowerment: The Art of Creating Your Life As You Want It* which has been translated into over fourteen languages, the critically acclaimed *The Rhythm of Compassion*, and the award-winning feminist memoir *Returning to My Mother's House*. She lives in the Hudson River Valley in New York.

www.empowermentinstitute.net
www.imagineprogram.net

ABOUT THE ARTIST

Kate McGloughlin is a celebrated painter and printmaker who currently lives and maintains a successful studio in Olivebridge, NY. She has been included in over seventy exhibitions in notable galleries and in four museums in the United States, Japan, and Ireland, and is currently president of The Woodstock School of Art where she teaches printmaking, landscape painting and directs the newly renovated printmaking studio. *Requiem for Ashokan*, a multimedia exhibition of paintings, prints, text and spoken word premiered at The Woodstock Artists Association & Museum in June 2017.

www.katemcgloughlin.com

HOMEBOUND PUBLICATIONS

Ensuring that the mainstream isn't the only stream.

At Homebound Publications, we publish books written by independent voices for independent minds. Our books focus on a return to simplicity and balance, connection to the earth and each other, and the search for meaning and authenticity. Founded in 2011, Homebound Publications is one of the rising independent publishers in the country. Collectively through our imprints, we publish between fifteen to twenty offerings each year. Our authors have received dozens of awards, including: *Foreword Reviews'* Book of the Year, Nautilus Book Award, Benjamin Franklin Book Awards, and Saltire Literary Awards. Highly-respected among bookstores, readers and authors alike, Homebound Publications has a proven devotion to quality, originality and integrity.

We are a small press with big ideas. As an independent publisher we strive to ensure that the mainstream is not the only stream. It is our intention at Homebound Publications to preserve contemplative storytelling. We publish full-length introspective works of creative non-fiction as well as essay collections, travel writing, poetry, and novels. In all our titles, our intention is to introduce new perspectives that will directly aid humankind in the trials we face at present as a global village.

WWW.HOMEBOUNDPUBLICATIONS.COM